ADVENTURES IN MISSING THE POINT

HOW THE CULTURE-CONTROLLED CHURCH NEUTERED THE GOSPEL

OTHER TITLES BY THESE AUTHORS

Brian D. McLaren

The Church on the Other Side (Zondervan)

Finding Faith (Zondervan)

A New Kind of Christian (Jossey-Bass)

More Ready Than You Realize (Zondervan)

The Story We Find Ourselves In (Jossey-Bass)

Tony Campolo

Revolution and Renewal: How Churches Are Saving Our Cities (Westminster/John Knox Press)

Let Me Tell You a Story (the W Group)

It's Friday, but Sunday's Coming (the W Group)

You Can Make a Difference (the W Group)

Can Mainline Denominations Make a Comeback? (Judson Press)

BRIAN D. MCLAREN & TONY CAMPOLO

ADVENTURES IN MISSING THE POINT

HOW THE CULTURE-CONTROLLED CHURCH NEUTERED THE GOSPEL

Adventures in Missing the Point: How the Culture-Controlled Church Neutered the Gospel
Copyright © 2003 by Youth Specialties

Youth Specialties Products, 300 S. Pierce St., El Cajon, CA 92020, are published by
Zondervan Publishing House, 5300 Patterson Ave. S.E., Grand Rapids, MI 49530

Library of Congress Cataloging-in-Publication Data

McLaren, Brian D., 1956-
  Adventures in missing the point : how the culture-controlled church
neutered the Gospel / by Brian D. McLaren and Tony Campolo.
    p. cm.
  ISBN 0-310-25384-5
  1. Theology, Doctrinal--Popular works.   I. Campolo, Anthony. II.
Title.
  BT77 .M388 2003
  270.8'3--dc21

2002156593

Edited by Tim McLaughlin
Design by Burnkit
Printed in the United States of America

05 06 07 / DCI / 10 9 8 7 6 5

A NOTE FROM THE PUBLISHER

The emergentYS line was created in response to the rising interest of church leaders and growing numbers of Christians regarding the emerging church and culture—and the profound changes the church is now facing. The emergentYS line will address the complex issues of our world's ongoing cultural shifts and the impact this will have on the local church and its ministries.

The purpose of emergentYS is to provoke thought and conversation. This line of resources will help navigate the way we work through theological issues and open up discussion on topics that are essential for many people. Welcome to the conversation!

www.emergentYS.com

ZONDERVAN™

GRAND RAPIDS, MICHIGAN 49530 USA

DEDICATIONS AND ACKNOWLEDGMENTS

Thanks to Youth Specialties and Zondervan for their hard work on this project. And thanks to Jo-Ann Badley for her insights into the story of Dinah in the chapter on the Bible. See www.emergentvillage.org if you're interested in more of Badley's stuff.

—*Brian D. McLaren*

In honor of Joe Modica, the chaplain of Eastern University, who never seems to miss the point when it comes to communicating the gospel.

—*Tony Campolo*

CONTENTS

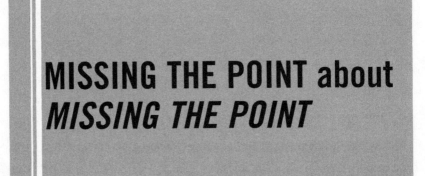

MISSING THE POINT about
MISSING THE POINT

Sometimes the first thing we forget is what we're really trying to do. At least that's what my friend Jim Henderson says, and he has a story to prove it:

I'M IN HOME DEPOT. A SERIES OF CONSUMER CANYONS TOWER MENACINGLY OVERHEAD. ALL I NEED IS A THINGAMAJIG. WHERE IS IT AND WHO CARES? MY EYES QUICKLY SCAN THE HORIZON OF STUFF LOOKING FOR A LITTLE JUST-IN-TIME CUSTOMER SERVICE.

I WANT TO SCREAM: TAKE YOUR EYES OFF THOSE BOXES! GET DOWN OFF THAT STUPID LADDER! QUIT VISITING WITH YOUR COWORKERS! DON'T PICK UP THAT PHONE! PAY ATTENTION TO ME!

BUT IT'S POINTLESS, AND I FINALLY GET IT: I'M AN INTERRUPTION. AN IRRITATION. THEY'D PREFER I WASN'T IN THEIR BUILDING.

THEY'VE FORGOTTEN WHY THEY WENT INTO BUSINESS. IT WASN'T TO COUNT BOXES. OR VISIT EACH OTHER. OR IGNORE THE CUSTOMER. THEY WENT INTO BUSINESS TO PAY ATTENTION TO THE CUSTOMER.

EMPLOYEES LIKE THESE HAVE MISSED THE POINT.

Which is how a lot of us feel about the way we're living out Christian faith in the early 21st century. Somehow, we're missing the point. We pastors and preachers listen to our own sermons, see the frantic pace of programs and meetings we've created, and shivers run up our spines: are we somehow missing the point?

Are our churches and broadcasts and books and organizations merely creating religious consumers of religious products and programs? Are we creating a self-isolating, self-serving, self-perpetuating, self-centered subculture instead of a world-penetrating (like salt and light), world-serving (focused on "the least and the lost," those Jesus came to seek and save), world-transforming (like yeast in bread), God-centered (sharing God's love for the whole world) counterculture? If so, even if we proudly carry the name *evangelical* (which means "having to do with the gospel"), we're not behaving as friends to the gospel, but rather as its betrayers. However unintentionally, we can neuter the very gospel we seek to live and proclaim. This book is our attempt, flawed and faltering to be sure, to get us thinking about the frightening possibility of unintentional betrayal of the gospel by those entrusted with it.

And more, this book isn't about pointing fingers at "them" for their mistakes. It's about us. Protestants and Catholics, liberals and conservatives, hand-clappers and nonclappers, Pentecostals and Presbyterians (and Pentecostal Presbyterians)—all of us.

So we'd like to invite all of us to consider ways that we're missing the point—to share a journey of (re)discovering what we're supposed to be about.

You won't find a blueprint in these chapters—no five easy steps, no new model to roll out. We're just two bald guys learning to love the Lord and the church and the world, and we're trying to figure out the point of being Christians. In the process we're becoming more and more aware of how often we miss the point ourselves. And on occasion in these pages, you'll see how each of us thinks the other might be missing the point as well! (And hopefully, you'll see us demonstrate a good-natured way of disagreeing, too.)

Every once in a while, muddling through life, we see things in a new, clearer light, and we're surprised by the epiphany.

Consider the case of Jason, a young college student who, during the time he was attending Brian's church, was diagnosed with schizophrenia. Soon after the diagnosis he rented a room in Brian's big house, like a few other single guys (without mental disorders) did.

Fast forward a few years. All the guys in Brian's house have moved out and got places of their own. One day Brian learns from a mutual friend that Jason is "normal" again. The two of them get together, and Brian immediately recognized that something was different: for starters, Jason called him Brian instead of Mr. McLaren, which for some reason he had called him since his illness had kicked in.

"Can you explain what I was like when I lived with you?" Jason asked Brian. "I feel like I just woke up from a dream and my whole past is like a fog. I'm trying to piece it together."

During the few hours they were together, Brian felt like he was watching *Awakenings*, seeing a miracle before his eyes.

But as in the movie, the miracle was short-lived, and Jason's schizophrenia gradually returned. It turned out that a new doctor had changed medications, and during the transition— when the effects of the old drug were waning and those of the new were increasing—Jason's brain chemistry returned to that fragile state we call "normal." Sadly, the doctor has never been able to recapture that fragile balance.

Like Jason during that brief period of clarity, we may be in a rare moment of opportunity as a culture. The waning of modernity and the rise of postmodernity may give us a few days or weeks of unusual clarity. We begin to realize what a fog we have been in, how we may have been missing the point. In such lucid moments we might find ourselves in the calm eye of a hurricane—an interlude of clear skies and gentle winds, of clear thinking and improved vision, where we can reassess our lives, re-imagine our future direction. And with any luck,

13

perhaps the pair of cultural influences—one waning and the other waxing—can somehow neutralize each other and somehow make our cultural awakening longer-lived.

But shame on you if you use this book to critique others, to point the finger and say, "See how *they're* missing the point!" If you do that, *you're* missing the point. This adventure is not about finding the splinter in someone else's eye, not about judging others for their poor vision.

Or if you get defensive while reading this book, thinking, *Hey, I'm not missing the point. You authors are missing the point. I see everything perfectly clearly*—if you think this, then you're missing more than the point: you're missing an opportunity to learn, to reflect, to grow. This adventure isn't about defending ourselves.

What this adventure is about is facing our own blindnesses, our own insanities, our own foggy thinking and clouded judgment. It's about admitting that we haven't seen things clearly, and about wanting to think more clearly than we do. Like the fellow in this story:

> *Then they came to Jericho. As Jesus and his disciples, together with a large crowd, were leaving the city, a blind man, Bartimaeus (that is, the Son of Timaeus), was sitting by the roadside begging. When he heard that it was Jesus of Nazareth, he began to shout, "Jesus, Son of David, have mercy on me!"*
>
> *Many rebuked him and told him to be quiet, but he shouted all the more, "Son of David, have mercy on me!"*
>
> *Jesus stopped and said, "Call him."*
>
> *So they called to the blind man, "Cheer up! On your feet! He's calling you." Throwing his cloak aside, he jumped to his feet and came to Jesus.*
>
> *"What do you want me to do for you?" Jesus asked him.*
>
> *The blind man said, "Rabbi, I want to see."*
>
> *"Go," said Jesus, "your faith has healed you." Immediately he received his sight and followed Jesus along the road.* (Mark 10:46-52)

We do not claim to see all that much. We're just rubbing our eyes and trying to be aware of where our perspective has been foggy. We're trying to wake up. Part of that waking up is to engage each other—and, hopefully, you—in a conversation. That's why each of our chapters is followed by a response from the other author—agreements, counterpoints, questions, additions. Join the conversation! Read this book with friends and talk about it together.

The adventure is for those who simply and passionately want to see. It's for those who have a passionate thirst for insight that won't be silenced by the polite crowds along the road. It's for those who, as they begin to see, want to follow Jesus along the road.

—*Brian* and *Tony*

GOD

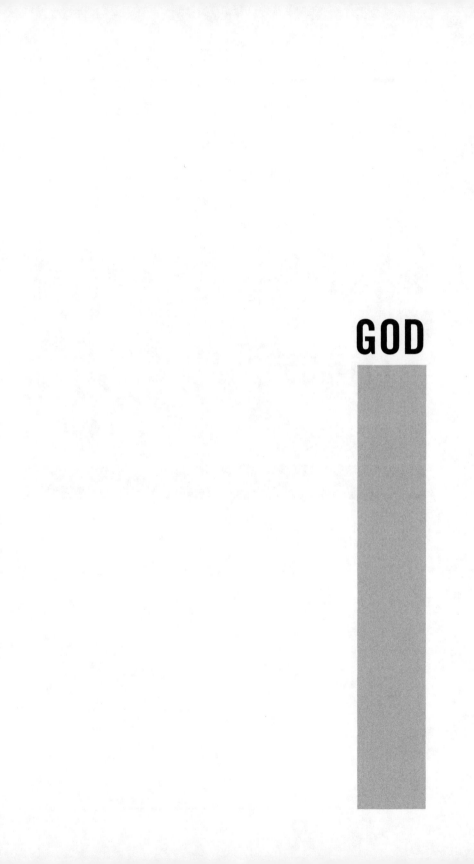

MISSING THE POINT:
Salvation

Brian D. McLaren

Are you saved?

For people who come from evangelical and fundamentalist backgrounds (as I do), life is about being (or getting) saved, and knowing it. I was taught that the ideal Christian could tell you the exact date—and maybe even the hour and minute—when he was saved, when he experienced salvation. *Are you saved?* was a question that everyone understood meant one or all of the following:

- You had accepted Jesus Christ as your personal Savior.

- You believed that Jesus died on the cross for your sins, and you believed his death, not your good deeds, made it possible for your sins to be forgiven.

- At the end of a church service, during the "invitation," you had said "the sinner's prayer," then during the "invitation" walked to the front of the church—this was the "altar call"—or perhaps only raised your hand to acknowledge your conversion.

- You gained an assurance that you were going to heaven after you died.

I assure you, I think it's good to be saved in this way. Yet I also think that the Bible has less to say about these four things than many Christians may think. Consider:

- The phrase *accept Christ as your personal Savior* is not in the Bible. Even *personal Savior* is absent from the pages of the Bible. In fact, the Bible seems to make the focus of salvation on *us* as a people, not on *me* as an individual.

- Having your sins forgiven is no doubt a part of (or a prelude to) salvation. But in the Bible salvation means much more than that: if anything, being forgiven is the starting line, not the finish line, of salvation.

19

- Nowhere in the Bible is the term *sinner's prayer* mentioned, and no one in the Bible ever says it—at least not in the form that prospective converts are taught to say it today. And it wasn't until the last 150 years or so that Christian services included "invitations" or "altar calls." Furthermore, no one has ever or will ever walk down an aisle or raise a hand to "get saved." Invitations, altar calls, and sinner's prayers are wonderful and often useful traditions or rituals—I just don't think that salvation lies in them.

- If you had asked the apostle Paul, "If you were to die tonight, do you know for certain that you would be with God in heaven?" I'm certain Paul would have said yes. But he probably would have given you a funny look and wondered why you were asking this question, because to him it missed the point. To Paul the point of being Christ's follower was not just to help people be absolutely certain they were going to heaven after they died. Paul's goal was to help them become fully formed, mature in Christ, here and now—to experience the glorious realities of being in Christ and experiencing Christ in themselves.

So if we are missing the point about salvation, what is the point?

For starters, in the Old Testament the Hebrew word that is translated *salvation* means *rescue*—especially rescue from sickness, trouble, distress, fear, or (this especially) from enemies and their violence. You see this meaning clearly in passages like this one, in which the people rejoice that God has saved them from the Egyptians who had violently oppressed them as slaves for generations:

The Lord is my strength and my song;
he has become my salvation.
He is my God, and I will praise him,
my father's God, and I will exalt him. (Exodus 15:2)

Or take David, who expresses the same joy over being rescued from violent people—in this case, King Saul:

My God is my rock, in whom I take refuge,
my shield and the horn of my salvation.
He is my stronghold, my refuge and my savior—
from violent men you save me. (2 Samuel 22:3)

A Jewish priest named Zacharias understood salvation in this same sense. At the birth of his long-awaited son (who would be known as John the Baptizer), Zacharias sang a song about salvation—but the enemies *he* sang about were certainly the Romans, who oppressed the Jewish people and denied them their full freedom:

He has raised up a horn of salvation for us
in the house of his servant David
(as he said through his holy prophets of long ago),
salvation from our enemies
and from the hand of all who hate us—
to show mercy to our fathers
and to remember his holy covenant,
the oath he swore to our father Abraham:
to rescue us from the hand of our enemies,
and to enable us to serve him without fear
in holiness and righteousness before him all our days. (Luke 1:69–75)

It's clear that in these passages the speakers aren't talking about being saved from hell. They're talking about being saved from the Egyptians, King Saul, the Romans—about being liberated from violence and oppression and the distressing fear they engender.

Not that being saved from hell is unimportant or unbiblical. It is only that I think we sometimes jump to that interpretation of *salvation* too quickly—and in so doing, we miss the full point of salvation.

For just a minute or two, box up your understanding of *salvation* and *saved* long enough to listen to a story, as if it were the first time you ever heard it.

Back in about 1400 B.C., the Bible tells us, the Jewish people were slaves in Egypt. They prayed for relief, and God sent them Moses, who led them to freedom. Moses didn't take the credit, though—he knew it was God who saved the people from slavery. After the people escaped Egypt and settled in Palestine, many of their neighbors would brutally attack them— the Philistines, the Amalekites, and others. Again and again, they would pray—and sure enough, God would send them a deliverer (or savior) to save them (or bring them salvation).

They eventually faced their most dangerous enemies of all. To their north and east, the powerful and brutal Assyrian empire attacked and destroyed Israel's northern tribes. Some years later the Assyrians were replaced by a Babylonian regime, and *they* attacked Israel's southern tribes. They prayed for salvation, but they were not spared. They weren't destroyed, either: many were carried away as exiles, or prisoners of war, to be used as servants in the Babylonian empire. When they arrived in Babylon, the Jews kept on praying for salvation—this time, salvation from their exile.

Later, yet another regime—the Medo-Persians—replaced the Babylonians, and the Hebrew exiles were allowed to return to their promised land of Israel. The Greeks soon ruled over Judea, and after the Greeks, the Romans. It seemed the Jews were destined to remain under the control of larger, more powerful empires.

When would their salvation come? When would their liberation come?

After many centuries, the question *When?* gave way to the more vexing question *Why?* Why didn't God save them this time? Their history was full of stories of God's salvation, but now he seemed deaf to their cries. Why?

A group of pious, devout people known as the Pharisees had an answer: the reason God didn't save the people from oppression (not from hell) was *because of their sins*. If the people would just become more holy and devout, then God would surely save them. The Pharisees dedicated themselves, therefore, to purity—not only for their own sake, but for the salvation of their people (from oppression and violence).

Perhaps for the first time, *sin* became a major concern—it was the answer to the *Why doesn't God rescue us?* question. The Pharisees consequently resented anyone who was obviously sinful: prostitutes (who sinned sexually), tax collectors (who cooperated with the oppressors), the drunks (who lacked self-discipline), the gluttons (who, unlike the Pharisees, didn't fast to prove their piety). "It's *their* fault we are oppressed," the Pharisees said. "It's *their* fault we are not being saved."

At last, an obvious answer to the *Why?* question.

Then came the remarkable conception of a young but faith-filled Jewish girl:

> But after [Joseph] had considered this, an angel of the Lord appeared to him in a dream and said, "Joseph son of David, do not be afraid to take Mary home as your wife, because what is conceived in her is from the Holy Spirit. She will give birth to a son, and you are to give him the name Jesus, because he will save his people from their sins." (Matthew 1:20–21)

Did you notice the profound shift? He will save his people from their *what*? For the first time in Jewish history, a promised salvation was not liberation from political oppression and religious persecution. Instead, as the angel informed Joseph, the rescue of people from their sins would be the prerequisite to any rescue from oppression. Save the people from their sins, as Gabriel promised that Jesus will do, and salvation from oppression would inevitably follow.

Can you see now why the Pharisees, who were working hard to pressure the obvious sinners to change their ways so the Messiah could come and bring salvation—can you see why they would be upset with Jesus? Instead of joining the Pharisees in their disdain for the supposed sinners, Jesus was kind to prostitutes, ate with tax collectors, spoke too much about forgiveness and not enough about judgment (except, ironically, when he was talking about the Pharisees), and was gracious even to Roman soldiers, Samaritans, and Syrophonecians. He *couldn't* be the Messiah. If anything, he was the anti-messiah. No wonder they wanted to kill him.

"You people are completely focused on political salvation of your people to the exclusion of everyone else," Jesus essentially told the Pharisees. "Don't you remember? God's promise to Abraham was not limited to Abraham's descendents: his promise was to bless Abraham and *make him a blessing*, to make Abraham's descendents a great nation, *so they could bless all other nations*. So by being preoccupied only with your own blessing, your own liberation, your own concerns—you are missing the whole point about salvation."

Jesus' message and manner infuriated the Pharisees, of course, turning their expectations to confetti.

"That's right," many modern Christians respond at this point. "Those Pharisees should have realized that Jesus came to save them spiritually from hell after death, not politically from the Romans in this life. They really missed the point."

I think, though, Jesus would then say to us, "No, *you're* missing the point, too. You're missing the point about why *they* missed the point."

Then we would be all confused, and then we would *really hear* what Jesus said to first-century Jews:

SALVATION DOESN'T MEAN SLITTING ROMAN THROATS
AND GETTING POWER. SALVATION MEANS BEING LIBER-
ATED FROM THE CYCLE OF VIOLENCE, LIBERATED FROM
THE NEED TO BE IN POWER. GOD WANTS TO SAVE YOU
FROM YOUR PRESENT LIFE OF HATRED AND FEAR, AND
INSTEAD RECONNECT YOU WITH GOD'S ORIGINAL PLAN
FOR THE DESCENDENTS OF ABRAHAM. EVEN AS AN
OPPRESSED PEOPLE, YOU CAN BE A BLESSING. INSTEAD
OF SLITTING A ROMAN SOLDIER'S THROAT, CARRY HIS
PACK FOR HIM. INSTEAD OF CURSING HIM, PRAY FOR
HIM. I AM HERE TO SAVE YOU FROM THE WHOLE SYSTEM
OF INSULT AND REVENGE—NOT BY GIVING YOU POLITI-
CAL VICTORY (AS YOU WISH I WOULD), AND NOT BY
TELLING YOU TO GIVE UP ON THIS LIFE AND INSTEAD
FOCUS ON SALVATION FROM HELL AFTER THIS LIFE (AS
SOME PEOPLE ARE GOING TO DO IN MY NAME)—BUT BY
GIVING YOU PERMISSION TO START YOUR PARTICIPATION
IN GOD'S MISSION RIGHT NOW, RIGHT WHERE YOU ARE,
EVEN AS AN OPPRESSED PEOPLE. THE OPPORTUNITY TO
START LIVING IN THIS NEW AND BETTER WAY IS AVAIL-
ABLE TO YOU RIGHT NOW: THE KINGDOM OF GOD IS AT
HAND!

So there's the ancient Jewish way of missing of the point
(thinking salvation is only about politics in the here and now)
and the modern Christian way of missing of the point (thinking salvation is only about escaping hell after you die). There's
another approach: that salvation means being rescued from
fruitless ways of life here and now, to share in God's saving
love for all creation, in an adventure called the kingdom of
God, the point of which you definitely don't want to miss.

Plus, of course, the wonderful gift of assurance that you will not perish after this life, but will be forever with the Lord.

Consider the Parable of the Race. Once upon a time, in a land of boredom and drudgery, exciting news spread: "There is going to be a race! And all who run this race will grow strong and they'll never be bored again!" Exciting news like this had not been heard for many a year, for people experienced little adventure in this ho-hum land, beyond attending committee meetings, waiting in lines, sorting socks, and watching sitcom reruns.

Excitement grew as the day of the race drew near. Thousands gathered in the appointed town, at the appointed place. Most came to observe, skeptical about the news. "It's too good to be true," they said. "It's just a silly rumor started by some teenaged troublemakers. But let's stick around and see what happens anyway."

Others could not resist the invitation, arriving in their running shorts and shoes. As they waited for the appointed time, they stretched and jogged in place and chattered among themselves with nervous excitement. At the appointed time they gathered at the starting line, heard the gun go off, and knew that it was time to run.

Then something very curious happened. The runners took a step or two or three across the starting line, and then abruptly stopped. One man fell to his knees, crying, "I have crossed the starting line! This is the happiest day of my life!" He repeated this again and again, and even began singing a song about how happy this day was for him.

Another woman started jumping for joy. "Yes!" she shouted, raising her fist in the air. "I am a race-runner! I am finally a race-runner!" She ran around jumping and dancing, getting and giving high fives to others who shared her joy at being in the race.

Several people formed a circle and prayed, quietly thanking God for the privilege of crossing the starting line, and thanking God that they were not like the skeptics who didn't come dressed for the race.

An hour passed, and two. Spectators began muttering; some laughed. "So what do they think this race is?" they said. "Two or three strides, then a celebration? And why do they feel superior to us? They're treating the starting line as if it were a finish line. They've completely missed the point."

A few more minutes of this silliness passed. "You know," a spectator said to the person next to her, "if they're not going to run the race, maybe we should."

"Why not? It's getting boring watching them hang around just beyond the starting line. I've had enough boredom for one life."

Others heard them, and soon many were kicking off their dress shoes, slipping out of their jackets, throwing all this unneeded clothing on the grass. And they ran—past the praying huddles and past the crying individuals and past the jumping high-fivers. And they found hope and joy in every step, and they grew stronger with every mile and hill. To their surprise, the path never ended—because in this race, there was no finish line. So they were never bored again.

Is salvation for you a one-time experience? Or is it a lifelong journey? Is it about rescue from your uncomfortable circumstances (as it was for the ancient Jews), or rescue from this world after death (as it is for many modern Christians)—or is it about being rescued from a life that is disconnected from God and God's adventure, both in this life and the next? Is salvation about stepping across a line—or is it about crossing a starting line to begin an unending adventure in this life and beyond?

Brian is on target when he contends that the salvation Jesus preached was primarily for the here and now. Life in the next world is *not* where the attention of Jesus was focused. What Jesus offered to people, Brian points out, was a spiritual transformation that would make them into a new kind of people—a people delivered from the animosities, fears, and guilt that drain life of its joys. The salvation that Christ offers involves becoming new persons who live out love and justice in the world.

It's not just for the elderly that salvation from the threat of death is a big deal. From early childhood, Ernest Becker contends in *Denial of Death*, the subconscious fear of death permeates the consciousness and is at the root of phobias that can render us psychologically dysfunctional. Young people are more threatened by death than most of them realize. When we talk about salvation, we must highlight not only the transformation experienced in this life, but also the good news that in Christ Jesus death itself has lost its sting.

Furthermore, I wonder if Brian isn't used to presenting salvation to sophisticated people, to whom Satan may be more of a caricature than a reality. Nevertheless, Satan is real, and evil is personified in him. We must beware of Satan being reduced to some little demon that sits on our shoulders and whispers nasty temptations into our ears. The Bible makes it clear that he is a seductive beast that raises havoc in our personal lives as well as being incarnated in the principalities and powers (i.e., the political and economic systems, the educational and familial systems, and the media) with which we must wrestle every day (Ephesians 6:12). Satan is a power that can nearly dominate human behavior, but in Christ we have the power to overcome the demonic: "The one who is in you is greater than the one who is in the world" (1 John 4:4). To those of us who are consciously aware that we are struggling against the demonic, it's good news that Christ saves us from the evil one and his legions.

Finally: yes, I concur with Brian's contention that being saved is not a simple once-and-for-all decision to accept some doctrinal statements. Yet I believe that Brian does readers a disservice when he does not emphasize that there is indeed a specific decision time in every person's life. Karl Barth declared—and I agree—that making an existential decision is key to becoming a Christian. Somewhere along the line, individuals must decide if they will make Jesus Lord of life—and that specific decision conditions all that is said and done from that moment forward.

As Brian himself writes, salvation is not just believing the doctrines. Salvation is a lifetime of asking, "What would Jesus do?" And don't let all those lapel pins diminish the importance of asking that question constantly. Whether it's going down the aisle of a crowded auditorium or down on one's knees by oneself in a solitary room, there comes a moment to decide.

MISSING THE POINT:
Theology

Tony Campolo

"You might be a sociologist," a critic of mine told me, "but you are certainly not a theologian."

Of course I am. Everyone is a theologian. Everybody has something to say about God. People can tell you why they believe what they believe. My critic can say that my theology is superficial or wrongheaded—but not that I am not a theologian. All of us carry with us what we believe and why we believe it. Even atheists are theologians, with specific ideas about a cosmos empty of any deity.

Just because grocery clerks or accountants or backhoe operators cannot label their theologies with four-syllable words doesn't mean they don't think deeply and often about God and the hereafter and the here-and-now and how they all fit together.

So let's demystify the word *theology*. A theology is a system of thought that enables us to answer the ultimate questions of our lives in reference to God.

- When we try to figure out what God expects us to do for a livelihood, and how that intersects our inner, spiritual life—we are formulating a theology of work.

- When we try to figure out our own sexual issues and problems, and compare them to what we understand of God's designs for sex and marriage—we are developing a theology of sexuality.

- When we try to determine our relationship to the environment, and what God requires of us in caring for it—we are developing a theology of nature.

- When facing the death of a loved one, a close friend, or even our own death, and struggle with understanding what life and death are all about, and what waits for us beyond time, matter, and space—we are developing an eschatology.

You get the point. We all have opinions and feelings about such ultimate concerns—and to that extent, we are all theologians.

That everyone has a theology, whether they call it that or not, is fact. It is also a fact, unfortunately, that our tendency is to absolutize our own theology, to convince ourselves that our neat little systems of belief we have constructed over the years is The Truth.

It's a short distance from "God's way is my way" to "My way is God's way" (not to mention "My way is Yahweh"). God is greater than any theology or system of ideas we come up with about God. God is not defined by our systems, by our theologies—not even by our firm convictions about him or her. Yes, *or her*—for God also transcends anything we think we know about masculinity and femininity. Check your New Testament Greek: against the masculine God the Father and Son, the Holy Spirit is referred to in the feminine gender. Even the Trinity defies the systematic packaging that theologies try to give it.

Far from any individual's theology being The Right One, in one sense all theologies are heresies. For theologies, like heresies, are major or minor distortions of the truth.

> *We know in part and we prophesy in part, but when that which is perfect is come, then that which is in part shall be done away.*
> (1 Corinthians 13:9-10).

In other words, what you believe may be partly correct, but is certainly not completely correct. The point? We must always be open to further insights that will give us fuller understanding of what God is all about.

Let's get one thing straight: the One Thing. The one certainty against which all our theologies are guesswork. "This one thing I know," the apostle Paul wrote: Jesus, and how his crucifixion delivered us from sin, and how his resurrection assures us of eternal life.

I believe these are unquestionable absolutes for all Christians—and perhaps the *only* absolutes. In the end, God's truth is not a theology, but a person. Our faith is not about Jesus Christ, not based on Jesus Christ—it *is* Jesus Christ.

But that's where the certainties end. Christians explain their personal encounters with Jesus differently. We have different ways of explaining how our personal relationship with God defines how we function in daily life.

And these explanations and questions are all theologies we use to answer life's big and little questions—which is why you could call theology an "answering" discipline. With the Bible, and under the influence of the living and spiritually present Jesus, we all try to answer not only our inner questions, but also questions that society throws at us.

Especially the social questions tend to change as times change. The questions raised by the John Calvins and Martin Luthers of five centuries ago are not our questions today. Neither the Desert Fathers nor the preaching theologians of the Great Awakening had much to say about abortion or corporate ethics. Certainly their insightful writings inform us as we erect our own theologies in this century; but every generation, ours included, needs to articulate a theology that answers its own unique questions and dilemmas. New times need new theologies.

Let's take a cursory look at two distinctive Christian theologies that were formulated in the last century in attempts to explain the relationship of God to very specific dilemmas.

Liberation Theology

Observing their people suffering from poverty and political oppression, Latin American theologians went to the Scriptures, reflected on them, and concluded that God is on the side of people who struggle for social and economic justice.

Which as a theology holds vastly different implications from those conceived by, say, Luther and Calvin—who pretty much agreed that rulers must be obeyed without question, in spite of injustices they impose on their subjects. And their theological descendents—especially those in evangelical churches—still cite the principle St. Paul articulated in his letter to the Romans: God has ordained those who rule, and any who oppose those rulers oppose God (13:1-2).

Among those who disagree with this thinking are theologians José Míguez Bonino and Juan Luis Segundo, who read the Bible through a different theological filter: in the Bible as well as in life they see the continual struggle of the poor and oppressed seeking justice from the rich and powerful, who typically oppose the aims of the disenfranchised populace. Liberation theology holds that in all such struggles, God sides with the poor and the oppressed, and against the rich and the powerful. Didn't God side with the enslaved Israelites against the powerful Egyptians? Don't the prophecies of Amos, Jeremiah, Micah, and others—liberation prophets, if you will—declare that the word of God is always against the rich oppressors, and on behalf of the victims of injustice? And in Jesus liberation theologians find their ultimate biblical example of one who came to "bring down the mighty and lift up those who are of low degree" (Luke 4:52).

On a trip to the Dominican Republic some years ago, in a slum on the edge of Santo Domingo, my students once saw a theology of liberation being formed before their very eyes. One Sunday morning we decided to attend mass, to be conducted by a priest whom we greatly admired. He had a reputation for doing incredible good among the people of his barrio.

My students and I arrived to discover it was a standing-room-only mass; we lined up against the back wall. A hundred more worshipers gathered *outside* the church, clustered at the open windows, straining to hear the mass inside.

There was a reason for the huge turnout, we discovered. The slum in which the people lived was scheduled to be bulldozed and a marina built on the site, to accommodate tourists' yachts. Of course, this meant that the barrio's thousands would lose the only homes they had, even if they were just cardboard and plywood. And there was no place for them to go.

So the priest had been negotiating with government leaders at the presidential palace, hoping to persuade them either to forego their plans to destroy this barrio or—and this was preferable—to provide the people with decent housing. That Sunday morning at mass the priest was to report the status of the government's plan: as of that week, the slum was still scheduled to be bulldozed, the priest's negotiating efforts notwithstanding.

The priest concluded his report. A young man stood up. "But what if all this talk comes to nothing, Father?" he asked in a desperate voice. "What if these negotiations lead nowhere? What will we do when they come with the bulldozers to level our homes?"

Before the priest answered, another young man on the other side of the sanctuary stood and shouted, "If they come with the bulldozers to destroy our homes, we will fight them!" Then again, even louder: "We will fight them to the death! Are you with me?" he asked, turning to the congregation. "Are you with me?"

"Yes! Yes! Yes!" the congregation shouted back. "We are with you!"

In the midst of this uproar, the priest raised his arms. "Silence!" he shouted. He then paced to the altar, lifted up the host and the wine—the body and blood of Christ—and turning to the people, said, "When they come with bulldozers to destroy our homes, and we go out to fight them, *He* will be with us, too!"

Needless to say, the students and I had a long discussion afterwards about all of this. While the kingdom of God would beat swords into plowshares and bring an end to violence, there was no question that in the struggle for justice, God sides with the poor and the oppressed against the strong and the powerful.

Black Theology

As African-Americans have toiled to define themselves outside the racism they have endured in this country, they have articulated a theology that empowers them in their struggle.

Black theologians such as James Cone and Cornel West find in the African-American community a strong propensity to identify with the ancient Israelites in their escape from Egyptian enslavement. In Yahweh they find a God who identifies with the poor and economically oppressed Jews, who—like African slaves in this country—lost much of their ethnic identity. In Yahweh Black theologians find a God who empowers the downtrodden of the world to stand up for their freedom and struggle against their oppressors. In the Old Testament prophets, they find models for today's prophetic voices to cry out against the inequities of wealth and social injustices.

And when Black theologians come to Jesus, they see a savior who does not only make a way for individual believers to gain eternal life—they see one who was numbered among the despised and rejected of the world. In Jesus they find one with whom they can identify.

It was undoubtedly one of the most dramatic sermons ever delivered at Eastern College. "Jesus was a nigger," began the visiting Black theologian, shocking his student audience into attention. Not that Jesus necessarily had black skin, he continued, for being a nigger had to do with what you were in the eyes of the world. The word refers to the downtrodden, he explained, the spat upon, the cursed, the humiliated, the rejected, the despised. This was the sense—the very real sense—in which Jesus was a nigger.

"There's no way you can read chapter 53 of Isaiah and *not* come to this conclusion," he said. That prophet writes that the Messiah would be despised and rejected, spat upon and cursed—and then *we* would hide our faces from him."

"You want to be like Christ?" He leaned into the lectern and spoke quietly. "Then you must become a nigger, too. You must be ready to empty yourself of the wealth, status, power that has marked your life. Because in the end, only niggers can be saved."

There is no end of theologies, because there is no end of people desiring to understand their struggles and God's role in them. There are gay theologies (see the works of John Boswell), Asian theologies (read Ahn Byung-Mu)—name the issue, and there is probably a theology that attempts to explain it.

Theologies—traditional theologies, novel theologies, your own theology—help explain God and God's work to a people's circumstances. The danger, however, is when a personal theology ends up as a purely subjective way of thinking about God, isolated from the body of historical Christian theologies. Which is why the Bible is so important. Although Scripture can be (and has been) interpreted in countless ways, it remains the sole authority to which all theologians must answer. In the end, all Christians need to make a biblical case for their own theological claims.

McLaren Responds

I love Tony's statement that "in one sense all theologies are heresies." You find a similar sentiment in a poem-prayer by C. S. Lewis, who begins by acknowledging his own limitation in prayer to know the One to whom he prays:

> He whom I bow to only knows to whom I bow
> When I attempt the ineffable Name, murmuring *Thou*...
> ("Footnote to All Prayers")

Lewis proceeds to acknowledge that when he says the Name of God, his best thoughts are mere fancies and symbols, which he knows "cannot be the thing thou art." Then with postmodern sensitivity, Lewis ponders the inadequacy of human language and perspective:

> And all men are idolators, crying unheard
> To a deaf idol, if Thou take them at their word.

Even as we pray, then, we must count on God to take our misguided arrows and magnetize them toward their goal. He concludes:

> Take not, oh Lord, our literal sense. Lord, in Thy great,
> Unbroken speech our limping metaphor translate.

Gregory of Nyssa expressed a similar theological humility centuries before: "Only wonder understands. Concepts create idols." This humility must be a starting point for us, if we don't want to miss Tony's point about theology.

When Tony discussed Latin American, gay, Asian, African-American, and African theologies (and feminist theologies could be included too), he spoke of the danger when a personal theology ends up as a purely subjective way of thinking about God, isolated from the body of historical Christian theologies.

But sometimes that "body of historical Christian theologies" hangs on to plainly wrong beliefs—and hangs on stubbornly, and for a long time. Cases in point:

- The church community, informed by historical Christian theology, didn't immediately validate Martin Luther's questioning of the pope's authority to sell indulgences.

- Neither did the tradition quickly welcome the writings of Copernicus and Galileo as they proposed a huge shift in the perception of the Christian worldview.

- Nor has the community at large immediately endorsed the kind of rethinking Tony himself engages in regarding homosexuality or women in leadership or the importance of ecology—all of which he articulates in this book.

It takes time for the church to widely accept a truth that contradicts traditionally held doctrines or practices. Allow Negroes in the church? Let women preach? Let those hippies bring their guitars and drums into worship? Let parishioners take both the bread *and* the wine? Believe that the earth rotates around the sun? Preach in the streets or fields? Send missionaries to the heathen? All these innovations horrified many of their first hearers. But over time, they were confirmed not only as permissible, but as good.

So new theological ideas—possibly including some you read in this book—deserve to be first heard, and then tested, sifted, considered carefully (as Paul wrote in 1 Thessalonians 5:21). That, at least, is the ideal. Sometimes the church errs by accepting new ideas uncritically; other times the church errs by rejecting new ideas without giving them a chance. Through it all, the church shows itself to be a learning community, seeking to remain humble and childlike in the presence of the great Teacher.

In another book I suggested that we think of theology as an art and a science. Few artists have said, "I have finally finished the definitive landscape. Everyone else can put their brushes away now." Most painters know that landscapes evoke multiple artistic expressions, and an artist's work is never done. If that's true of a painted landscape, how much more is it true of the Creator of all actual landscapes, known and unknown?

Like art, scientific knowledge is hardly rigid and stable, but fluid, flexible, dynamic, like a spider's web. Scientists are constantly questioning and reworking traditional theories, proposing new ones, overturning last year's models for still better ones. Just as new data requires rethinking of old formulations, so our theological constructions must remain flexible, open to correction and expansion and reconception. If, as C. S. Lewis said, "All prayers blaspheme," then surely Tony is right about all theologies being, in a sense, heresies. Our goal? Not absolute and arrogant certainty about our theologies, but a proper and humble confidence in God.

MISSING THE POINT:
Kingdom of God

Tony Campolo

I ask students why Jesus came into the world, and I typically get answers like this:

- To seek and to save the lost

- To reveal God to us

- To provide us with a model for being fully human

- To defeat the demonic spirits of this world

Good answers, all of them. But I seldom hear a student repeat the mission statement that Jesus himself gave us. In the three synoptic Gospels, Jesus tells us that he has come first and foremost to declare that the kingdom of God is at hand. Many of his parables were about this kingdom: God's kingdom could be likened to a good seed that a farmer sows into the ground, Jesus pointed out, or to a mustard seed, or to a treasure buried in a field. With such analogies Jesus tried to convey to his disciples some understanding of the nature of his kingdom.

And God wants this kingdom to become established *on earth, now!* "Your kingdom come, your will be done, on earth as it is in heaven," Jesus taught his disciples to pray (Matthew 6:10). Which, of course, contradicts what both evangelicals and neo-Marxists believe about Christianity being an otherworldly, pie-in-the-sky-when-you-die religion that promises us mansions in the next world if only we endure the oppressions, inequities, and injustices of the present socioeconomic order.

God's kingdom is a new society that Jesus wants to create in *this* world—within human history, not after the Second Coming or a future apocalypse or anything else. But right now.

The Old Testament describes this kingdom in several places, among them Isaiah 65:17-25:

> *For I am about to create new heavens and a new earth;*
> *the former things shall not be remembered or come to mind,*
> *But be glad and rejoice forever in what I am creating;*

for I am about to create Jerusalem as a joy, and its people as a delight.
I will rejoice in Jerusalem, and delight in my people;
  no more shall the sound of weeping be heard in it, or the cry of distress.
No more shall there be in it an infant that lives but a few days,
  or an old person who does not live out a lifetime;
For one who dies at a hundred years will be considered a youth,
  and one who falls short of a hundred will be considered accursed.
They shall build houses and inhabit them;
  they shall plant vineyards and eat their fruit.
They shall not build and another inhabit;
  they shall not plant and another eat;
For like the days of a tree shall the days of my people be,
  and my chosen shall long enjoy the work of their hands.
They shall not labor in vain, or bear children for calamity;
  for they shall be offspring blessed by the Lord — and their descendants
  as well.
Before they call I will answer, while they are yet speaking I will hear.
The wolf and the lamb shall feed together, the lion shall eat straw like the ox;
  but the serpent — its food shall be dust!
They shall not hurt or destroy on all my holy mountain, says the Lord.

Look at the details in this passage about the kingdom:

- Its coming will abolish all suffering.

- There will be an end to the infant mortality that is now so common among the poor.

- The elderly will live out their lives in good health.

- People will have decent housing that they can call their own.

- Everyone will have a job that pays to each a fair wage.

- Mothers will not worry when their children are born that they will be destroyed by drugs or blown away in gang warfare.

- The ecological balance of Eden will be restored, and environmental destruction will come to an end.

Elsewhere in the Old Testament—such as in Zechariah 8:4-5—we read that the neighborhoods of our cities will be safe, so that old people will be able to come out of their houses in the evenings, sit on their front steps, lean on their canes, and watch children playing in the streets.

And of course, the New Testament book of Revelation has plenty to say about this kingdom:

> And I heard a loud voice from the throne saying, "See, the home of God is among mortals. He will dwell with them as their God; they will be his peoples, and God himself will be with them; He will wipe every tear from their eyes. Death will be no more; mourning and crying and pain will be no more, for the first things have passed away."
>
> And the one who was seated on the throne said, "See, I am making all things new." Also he said, "Write this, for these words are trustworthy and true." (Revelation 21:3-5)

The desire to establish the kingdom of God on this earth has played a formative role in American history in particular. From our earliest days to the present, Americans have aspired to make their nation into God's kingdom here on earth (see H. Richard Niebuhr's, *The Kingdom of God in America*).

In the 17th century John Winthrop cherished this hope as he headed the Massachusetts Bay Colony, that Puritan society in the New World would be the "city built on a hill" that Jesus spoke of.

Eighteenth- and 19th-century evangelists and revivalists—like Charles Finney, for example—preached that with Christ's help, humanity could achieve a perfectionism that would lead to the biblically prophesized Millennium. American attempts at Utopian communities—be they the Oneida colonies of John Humphrey Noyes or the New Harmony communities of Robert Owen—witnessed the deep desire of Americans to live out the values and lifestyle of God's kingdom in the here and now. Even if you discount those who lived on the communal fringe of American society, the bulk of Americans firmly believed that our country had a manifest destiny ordained by the God of history.

At the turn of the 20th century, this optimistic outlook spawned the upbeat theology of the "Social Gospel," which held that the kingdom of God could be ushered into this world, without the return of Christ, through human effort. Christians filled with the Spirit of Jesus could bring in the new age of God's rule on earth. According to the Social Gospel, remarked H. Richard Niebuhr, "a God without wrath brought men without sin into a kingdom without judgment through the ministrations of a Christ without a cross." Believing that the human race was caught up in an evolutionary process that would carry it onward and upward, Social Gospel theologians and their followers were convinced that humanity was on the verge of outgrowing the selfishness and lusts that had always caused wars and pestilences in the past.

Then came two World Wars, which exploded the myth of moral progressivism, revealing instead the inherent evil in our humanity. Christian thought then adopted a view of the kingdom that could be reconciled with the apparently inevitable horror and destruction of this world: before the kingdom of God could become a historical reality, people needed to be radically transformed into the likeness of Christ. And that transformation could not be finally complete until Christ returned and made it happen (1 John 3:2).

This hard-nosed realism made it easy to resign oneself to believing that social progress was impossible—which is exactly what fundamentalists did. Followers of the Dispensationalist John Darby—and of the Scofield Reference Bible, which popularized Darby's Dispensational theology—believed that attempts to eliminate wars and poverty were a waste of time. Didn't the Scriptures say there would always be wars and rumors of wars (Mark 13:7), and that the poor we would always have with us (Matthew 26:11)? Dispensationalists—that is, fundamentalist and most evangelicals—contended that the world was a sinking ship, and that time and efforts were better spent trying to get people off the ship and saved before it went under. The ship would only sink lower in the water, and the world would only get worse and worse, until things got so bad that God would have to intervene, bringing its degradation to an end with the Second Coming of Christ.

The only problem, however, was how such bad news could really be the Good News. I remember sitting in church one Sunday night in my childhood, listening to an evangelist cite a torrent of sins that were flooding society—increasing crime rates, divorce rates, promiscuity among young people. As the evangelist preached his ominous warning, I could hear an elderly woman in the pew behind me moaning, "Thank you, Jesus! Maranatha, Lord, Maranatha!" After the service I asked my mother why this old saint was thankful for so much bad news. With the world going from bad to worse, my mother explained, it was all evidence to the elderly parishioner that the return of Christ was at hand. And most evangelicals still hold this view.

Over the years, I have come to believe that both the liberal Social Gospelers *and* the Dispensational Fundamentalists were each partly right. I now affirm the optimism of those who believe that God is at work in the world through faithful servants, both inside the church and outside the church, bringing hope to the poor, liberation to the oppressed, and the creation of a new society in which love and justice reign.

At the same time, however—even as I join with them in striving to realize this kingdom of God on earth—I also believe that we should not delude ourselves into thinking that whatever we can build of God's kingdom now can come to fullness without Christ's return. We are all flawed people, and only a face-to-face encounter with the eschatological Christ can make us into kingdom people. And without kingdom people, there is no kingdom—as John Milton wrote in *Paradise Lost*, "The mind is its own place, and in itself can make a Hell of Heaven and a Heaven of Hell." The conversion of individuals is indeed a prerequisite to the coming of the kingdom of God on earth.

Still, in the meantime we should be committed to pressing *toward* this kingdom—toward becoming what Jesus is calling us to be (Philippians 3:13-14). Remember: the whole creation is waiting for us to be instruments of God, through which it will be delivered from its present tragic condition (Romans 8:18-22).

So this is the tension: granted, we will not be like Christ until we are with him at his coming—yet we must daily press toward that goal, socially and civically as much as personally and spiritually. We may not be able to create the kingdom of God in its fullness prior to his return, yet we are nonetheless called by God to work *toward* that end. Which is the gist of what Paul wrote to the Philippians:

> *The one who began a good work among you will bring it to completion by the day of Jesus Christ.* (1:6)

Think of this tension this way. You are in France, and it is early 1944. Most of the country is occupied by the Nazi army. The Resistance is sabotaging German operations here and there, enough to disrupt and distract, but never enough to actually drive Hitler's forces out of France. What rifles and explosives have been smuggled to the Underground are nothing compared to the artillery and tanks of the Wehrmacht.

Looking only at the continent, seeing only a handful of ragged saboteurs armed with little more than determination and a willingness to die for their country—knowing only this, you would have no idea that at that moment across the English

Channel, there was being assembled the most massive invasion force in human history. And that within only a few months, the signal would be given to launch that force. And that shortly after that, Allied soldiers would finish what the French Resistance had started, and drive the Nazis out of France once and for all.

So it will be with God's people. Even as you and I struggle to take very small steps in creating the kingdom of God in the here and now, a huge invasion force is being gathered beyond the clouds. And, at an unexpected moment in history, a trumpet will sound, and Jesus will return with a mighty army to overthrow the evils of this present age. On that day Jesus will join our limited efforts and carry us to victory (Ephesians 1:18-22). Then justice will roll down like a mighty flood, and the kingdoms of this world will become the kingdoms of our God, and God shall reign forever and ever.

For a biblical image of this scenario, read the story Jesus told:

> The kingdom of heaven may be compared to someone who sowed good seed in his field; but while everybody was asleep, an enemy came and sowed weeds among the wheat, and then went away. So when the plants came up and bore grain, then the weeds appeared as well.
>
> And the slaves of the householder came and said to him, "Master, did you not sow good seed in your field? Where, then, did these weeds come from?"
>
> He answered, "An enemy has done this."
>
> The slaves said to him, "Then do you want us to go and gather them?"
>
> But he replied, "No; for in gathering the weeds you would uproot the wheat along with them. Let both of them grow together until the harvest; and at harvest time I will tell the reapers, 'Collect the weeds first and bind them in bundles to be burned, but gather the wheat into my barn.'"
>
> (Matthew 13:24-30, NRSV).

The tares represent the kingdom of evil, which is increasing in size and strength right up until the end of this present age. But look—the wheat, representing the kingdom of God, *also* is growing in size and strength as we approach the end time. So that at the return of Jesus, the kingdom of God will roll right over the kingdom of evil and become what it was aiming at all along.

Believe it or not, U2's lead singer Bono is using his wealth and celebrity status to do just that: increase the kingdom of God in the here and now. Even back in 1982 he was part of the Live Aid and Band-Aid concerts, whose earnings helped Ethiopians suffering through famine. Not content to merely help raise money with his performances, Bono was compelled to go to Ethiopia himself to ensure that the funds so raised were used honestly and effectively.

What he saw there changed his life. For six weeks he and his wife worked in an orphanage. "You wake up in the morning, and the mist would be lifting," he reminisces. "You'd walk out of your tent and you'd count bodies of dead or abandoned children. Or worse, the father of a child would walk up to you and try to give you his living child and say, 'You take it, because if this is your child, it won't die.'"

Bono has done more than continue contributing financially to the needs he saw firsthand nearly two decades ago. He now works fiercely to change the policies of governments and of organizations like the World Bank and the International Monetary Fund—in order that funding for public health, education, and essential social services will *increase* rather than decrease, as they have done lately. Politicians with views as diverse as Bill Clinton and Jesse Helms have taken Bono seriously and joined him in successful efforts to reduce Third World debts. He has persuaded wealthy countries to lend their financial muscle to addressing the AIDS crisis in Africa, thus saving tens of thousands from death.

However unlikely you think it is for a rock star to be an instrument of God, Bono has all the marks of one. He is changing the here-and-now world, doing what he can to move it toward the kingdom of God.

As much as individuals like Bono can do, it is the body of Christ—the church, the corporate body of believers—that is the ultimate means for this task. What Jesus began two millennia ago, we his body carry on until he comes again. It doesn't matter that this body of Christ is imperfect, composed as it is of humans who still spend their days and nights working out what it means to be Christian. At our best, we are trying to become a sanctified fellowship that stands over and against the dominant culture with its values and lifestyle. At our worst, we are a bickering, judgmental bunch. It doesn't matter: we are still God's best chance at showcasing what the whole world will become when the kingdom of God becomes fully actualized.

We are not unlike Nova Hutta, a socialist utopian city founded by Polish communists following World War II. In *The Secular City* Harvey Cox describes Nova Hutta as envisioned: decent housing and health services for everyone...excellent schools for all children...parks with trees and fountains scattered throughout the city...full employment for its work force...non-existent crime...elder care that preserved their dignity.

Nova Hutta was to be a perfect city, a demonstration to the rest of Poland of what waited for them when the nation was finally transformed into a pure communist state, in which nothing was privately held, but all citizens shared everything. Nova Hutta was a taste of that future. Better than any speech or promotional pamphlet, Nova Hutta would demonstrate the character of the world that was around the corner.

Nova Hutta, needless to say, did not live up to the ideal. Ironically, Poland did indeed follow the example of Nova Hutta, and with a vengeance: 30 years later, the Polish

Solidarity movement began eroding the power of European Communism, resulting a decade later in the dissolution of the Soviet Union itself.

Yet what Nova Hutta was *intended* to do is exactly what the church of Jesus Christ is to do in our world: be one community in the world that demonstrates what the entire world will one day be like. We should be a people bound together in Christian love who are cultivating a social system that attempts to incarnate what the kingdom will be like when it comes on earth, as it already is in heaven.

McLaren Responds

If our theologies make us focus only on the eternal and the individual (i.e., getting my soul into heaven) so that we avoid God's concern for the historic and the global (i.e., God's will being done on earth as well as in heaven), then the more people we win over to our theologies, the fewer people will care about God's world here and now.

The more converts we make, the worse the world will become.

If God really cares about justice in this world here and now, and if we are converting people away from that concern, then we are working against God. We could inadvertently become enemies of God's wishes.

Does this possibility frighten you? Do you dismiss it too quickly?

One of the toughest challenges we face, I believe, is to discover an understanding of the gospel that comprises historic and the eternal, individual and the global. The phrase *kingdom of God*, I believe, was Jesus' image intended to bring the historic, eternal, individual, and global together. May God help us to seek God's kingdom in *all* of its dimensions.

53

MISSING THE POINT:
End Times

Tony Campolo

One of the most decisive battles of World War II—and perhaps of the century—was the Normandy Invasion of June 6, 1944. On D-Day the outcome of the war was at stake. If the Nazi army could have driven the invading Allies back into the sea, victory for Hitler and the Third Reich would have been assured. But if the Allied forces could establish a beachhead at Normandy, their triumph in the war would be virtually inevitable. It would take nearly a year of bloody fighting, miserable conditions, and the deaths of tens of thousands of Allied soldiers—but victory did come. V-Day followed D-Day.

The cosmic battle between God and demonic forces also had its D-Day, and will have its V-Day. When the God-Man hung on the cross, all the dark forces of the universe zeroed in on him. At the D-Day of Calvary, God had become vulnerable, and the dark forces knew it. If there was ever a time when darkness could extinguish the light of the world, it would be then, when Jesus had allowed himself in love to be the victim of sin and injustice. And when that horrendous Friday was over, it did indeed appear that the demonic forces had triumphed.

Yet the third day witnessed a coup when Jesus broke the power of sin and death with his resurrection. This D-Day triumph ensured that, in the end, he would subdue all rebellious principalities and powers and establish his unchallenged rule over all and everything.

The D-Day victory of Jesus' resurrection by no means meant there would be no more suffering. There would be plagues and AIDS, famine and cancer, deliberate evil and accidental tragedies, massive Holocausts and personal anguish. The list of horrors would be long—but it would not be endless. For God's D-Day meant that V-Day would come. Guaranteed.

And that V-Day will be the Second Coming.

Although the Second Coming is a certainty—Christ *will* return, and the kingdoms of this world will then become the kingdom of our God—Jesus himself said that it is futile to pinpoint its precise date. As he told his disciples,

> *Truly I tell you, this generation will not pass away until all these things have taken place. Heaven and earth will pass away, but my words will not pass away. But about that day and hour no one knows, neither the angels of heaven, nor the Son, but only the Father. For as the days of Noah were, so will be the coming of the Son of Man. For as in those days before the flood they were eating and drinking, marrying and giving in marriage, until the day Noah entered the ark, and they knew nothing until the flood came and swept them all away, so too will be the coming of the Son of Man. Then two will be in the field; one will be taken and one will be left. Two women will be grinding meal together; one will be taken and one will be left. Keep awake therefore, for you do not know on what day your Lord is coming.* (Matthew 24:34-42).

Yet Christians have spent the last 2,000 years guessing at the season, the year, even the very date of the Second Coming. The apostle Paul—who expected the imminent return of Christ—had to warn the Christians of his day to get on about their business, for apparently some were spending all their time waiting for Christ's return instead of working and earning a living for themselves and their dependents. No freeloading, Paul declared (2 Thessalonians 3:10).

More date-guessing was indulged in by some early Christians, who thought they caught a clue in these words of Jesus to Peter, about John the "beloved disciple":

> *"If I want him to remain alive until I return, what is that to you? You must follow me." Because of this, the rumor spread among the believers that [John] would not die. But Jesus did not say that he would not die; he only said, "If I want him to remain alive until I return, what is that to you?"* (John 21:22-23).

These verses implied to early Christians that Christ would return before John would die. Add to this belief the fact that John actually did outlive the other disciples and died a natural death on the Mediterranean island of Patmos sometime during the last quarter of the first century. Needless to say, these

Christians held their breath with expectancy as John's life ebbed away.

Christians have been date-guessing ever since. Today fortunes have been amassed by Bible preachers from supposedly reading the signs of the times—signs that are usually recent and current events, particularly in the Middle East, events that supposedly must occur before the Second Coming itself.

Yet this reasoning, this interpretation runs counter to what Jesus said: *everything that had to be fulfilled before the Second Coming would be fulfilled before his generation died out.* Even Paul expected the return of Christ in his immediate future. Yet modern prophecy preachers imply that Paul didn't understand the Scriptures as well as they do, and that of course Jesus could not have returned in the first century—not before any one of several events of the 20th and 21st centuries that prophecy preachers point to as prerequisites of the Second Coming.

Such an assumption is arrogant. I believe that Paul was not mistaken and that modern prophecy preachers are inflating current happenings in the world with a prophetic significance that is utterly unbiblical.

The most widely preached interpretation of the Second Coming today, and certainly the interpretation held in some form by most evangelical churches, is Dispensationalism. It is an eschatology that was formulated relatively recently, that is reflected in the footnotes of the Scofield Reference Bible, and that forms the plot line of the wildly popular *Left Behind* series by Tim LaHaye and Jerry Jenkins. Dispensationalism first appeared in Christian writing and thinking during the 19th-century ministry of John Darby of Plymouth, England. For it was Darby who drafted the theology of Dispensationalism, and with it the idea of a pretribulation rapture.

The end times according to Darby's Dispensationalism predict that there will come a moment when Christians will instantaneously and simultaneously disappear from the earth and meet with Jesus somewhere high above the earth. This "rapture" will be followed by seven years of suffering for those who are left behind (hence the name of the LaHaye-Jenkins book series). Darby labeled these seven increasingly horrific years as the "Tribulation." During the Tribulation 188,000 Jews will not only accept Jesus as their Messiah, but will publicly witness about him to the rest of the human race remaining on earth.

Jesus returns to earth at the end of the seven-year Tribulation—this is the Second Coming (*to* earth this time, as opposed to *above* the earth at the Rapture)—to bind the powers of Satan, and establish his kingdom here on earth. The kingdom will endure for a thousand years—hence its name, the "Millennium"—after which Satan will be released for a short time to raise more of his evil havoc, and then finally be cast into a lake of fire for eternal damnation.

Darby, Scofield, LaHaye, et al., have no dearth of Bible passages that apparently support this specific and elaborate future timeline. Most evangelical Bible schools and colleges teach it as the correct biblical interpretation of the End Times—despite the fact that this interpretation has been around less than 150 years.

Contrary to Darby, Christianity has historically believed in general what the Apostles Creed declares: that Christ will come again "to judge the quick and the dead"—that is, a single event, a climactic and purposeful end. It has traditionally been perceived as a time when Christ would return, join the efforts of his people who were trying to bring in a just social order called the kingdom of God, and thereby bring those attempts to a glorious completion (Philippians 1:6). This is what was and is being taught by most mainstream theologians, from Augustine and John Calvin through Jürgen Moltmann and Karl Barth, and what most of Christendom holds even now.

Dispensationalism posits a world that is spiraling down morally…a world from which God removes first his own Holy Spirit and then his besieged and nearly defeated Christians so that he can finally judge unbelievers apocalyptically and lethally. This is a theology that—with its implicit threat of being left behind, of time running out—is used by Dispensational preachers to great evangelistic effect. It has been a very effective goad to conversion.

To the contrary, the history of the world is infused with the presence of God, who is guiding the world toward becoming the kind of world God willed for it to be when it was created. Human history is going somewhere wonderful. And those of us who struggle and suffer to help take it there are confident that as surely as Jesus defeated death and the devil on D-Day, so a V-Day is inevitable: the war will eventually be won. Rather than the Dispensational idea of fighting battles in a war that ultimately goes so bad that Christians must be raptured out of it, the Second Coming promises that if we do not grow weary in well doing, in due season we shall reap (Galatians 6:9).

Not that I disbelieve in prophesying. It's only that when the word is used in the New Testament, it means to preach the message of God—to *tell forth* rather than to *foretell*. If you want to prophesy as the New Testament describes it, you will tell people what God expects of them—not make specific predictions about the Second Coming based on esoteric interpretations of recent or current events.

Case in point: let me revisit an ancient, time-tested interpretation of Revelation, a book usually at the center of most modern prophecy preachers—an interpretation that is based not on prediction of political events that are prerequisite to the Rapture, but on telling forth the clear message of the New Testament to our modern world.

There is an intriguing description of two cities in Revelation 17: one city is called Babylon; the other, Jerusalem. Most biblical theologians agree that Babylon refers to the *dominant culture in which Christians find themselves living*. To first-century Christians, that was the Roman Empire. When early Christians spoke of the empire, they avoided arrest as unpatriotic subversives by speaking about "Babylon" instead of about their own literal "Rome." The Christian community in the ancient Mediterranean world understood this code.

Each age and each nation has had its own Babylon—its own dominant culture in which its Christians live. For 21st-century Americans, our dominant culture—our Babylon, our own materialistic, success-oriented, consumeristic society—is our own United States of America. As ancient Christians were called to live countercultural lives in opposition to the seductive influences of their dominant culture, so we Christians in modern America are called to be a countercultural people in the context of our own Babylon.

Revelation tells us some things about a people's Babylon. First, it demands worship. Babylon is essentially idolatrous. One's own dominant culture assumes the qualities of a deity among its citizens. The U.S. is no different: we are encouraged to follow the example of our founding fathers, who in the Declaration of Independence pledged to their new nation their lives, their fortunes, and their sacred honor. The book of Revelation suggests that patriotism like this can easily slip into idolatry—that people who may be reluctant to lay down their possessions for Christ are often ready and willing to give their very lives for America.

Don't get me wrong. I love America. I could not write this way in most other nations without facing imprisonment, or worse. I believe that America is the best Babylon on the face of the earth—but in the end, it is Babylon nevertheless. And as surely as Chaldea and Persia and Rome did, America is subtly, relentlessly working to shift our allegiance from Christ to it.

Babylon is not only idolatrous. It is also a whore who seduces (Revelation 17:1-6), a social system that lures us into craving what she has to sell us. So powerful are her allurements that we are prone to sacrifice the well-being of our families, to compromise our spiritual values, and to exhaust our energies— just to gratify our lusts she promises to satisfy.

What better description can there be for how our consumeristic society exercises its spell upon us? Ours is a society, claimed the radical sociologist Herbert Marcuse, that has seduced us into a slavery that is so attractive, comfortable, and titillating that we do not recognize it as slavery. We lust after what it offers to sell us without noticing what these lusts are doing to us. So powerful are its seductions that we end up desiring the gratifications of "the great whore" more than our authentic human needs. We readily trade intimacy with our families, our commitments to our God, our psychological and physical health—all for a shot at earning enough money to buy things "the great whore" offers for sale.

The whore Babylon seduces through marketing—flashing Internet ads, TV commercials, billboards and magazine ads. We are seduced into believing Calvin Klein will make us sexually attractive, that a Lexus will improve our image, that drinking Pepsi will guarantee our youthfulness. The Bible may ask why we spend our money on what doesn't satisfy us (Isaiah 55:2), but the Babylon of our culture tricks us into believing that buying and consuming and amassing is what *really* satisfies.

The consumerism that Babylon has seduced us into has horrendous consequences. Americans are only six percent of the world's population, yet we consume 43 percent of the world's resources. Not only are we obscene in our depletion of nature, but we do it at the expense of the other peoples of the world who lack what is needed for even bare sustenance. While Americans suffer from obesity, a billion people live with constant hunger.

Ironically, the book of Revelation also describes our cultural consumption, listing the natural resources we require to feed our lifestyle:

> ...cargo of gold, silver, jewels and pearls, fine linen, purple, silk and scarlet, all kinds of scented wood, all articles of ivory, all articles of costly wood, bronze, iron, and marble. (18:12-13)

A society whose "merchants of the earth" profit from exploiting their markets is doomed to collapse. In this sense the prophecy of Scripture is dead accurate: if Babylon does not repent, continuing instead to pursue its consumeristic and consumptive ways, its downfall is inevitable.

When Babylon finally does fall, the Bible predicts two reactions: the merchants will weep, and the saints will rejoice (Revelation 18:11; 19:1-2).

When their system collapses, business and commercial leaders whose lucrative trading sustained Babylon will weep because all of their financial investments will have disappeared. As they watch their system go up in smoke, they will weep not just for the horrendous loss of life, but for the economic consequences of the disaster.

> For in one hour all this wealth has been laid waste! And all shipmasters and seafarers, sailors and all whose trade is on the sea, stood far off and cried out as they saw the smoke of her burning, "What city was like the great city?" And they threw dust on their heads, as they wept and mourned, crying out, "Alas, alas, the great city where all who had ships at sea grew rich by her wealth! For in one hour she has been laid waste. Rejoice over her, O heaven, you saints and apostles and prophets! For God has given judgment for you against her." Then a mighty angel took up a stone like a great millstone and threw it into the sea, saying "With such violence Babylon the great city will be thrown down, and will be found no more; and the sound of harpists and

minstrels and of flutists and trumpeters will be heard in you no more; and an
artisan of any trade will be found in you no more; and the sound of the
millstone will be heard in you no more; and the light of a lamp will shine in
you no more; and the voice of bridegroom and bride will be heard in you no
more; for your merchants were the magnates of the earth, and all nations
were deceived by your sorcery" (Revelation 18:17-23, NRSV).

The merchants will weep, but the saints will rejoice at the
fall of Babylon the seductive culture. Angels too rejoice at the
collapse of Babylon. Together they shout hallelujah at the
collapse of the great whore. The social system that deceived so
many and brought such suffering to innocent people is no
more. Jesus has warned us, after all, to lay up not the kind of
treasures that moth and rust ruin, or that can be stolen,
swindled, or devalued—but rather to lay up treasures in heaven.
When Babylon falls, then, saints lose nothing, for they have
invested elsewhere: the kingdom of God.

Opposing the idolatrous city of Babylon is the new kingdom
that John labels *Jerusalem*. Again, as with John's use of *Babylon*,
we are dealing with a code word: to ancient Christians, it was a
reference to the new society that Christ was creating through
the church. This new social order, this new Jerusalem, was
envisioned by prophets that predated Jesus. It is the city that
Abraham longed to see when he left Ur of the Chaldees. It is
the dream that Isaiah described when he saw a city in which
there would be no poverty. Where everyone would have a
decent job and a decent house. Where infant mortality would
be unknown, and where parents would not fear when children
were born that their lives were headed toward calamity (Isaiah
65:17ff). "Jerusalem" is the kind of society that Jesus promised
when he declared the Jubilee, the city in which the poor would
have good news, the oppressed would be set free, and the
broken-hearted would be healed (Luke 4:18-19). This
"Jerusalem" is the social system that the whole of history points

toward, that is in fact the very goal of history—a kingdom that will be realized at Christ's physical return.

In short, this is what the Second Coming of Jesus is all about: ultimate hope...the fulfillment of all our dreams...the realization of every utopian expectation.

The Second Coming is not a threat, but a promise. It was given to us that we might have hope. It is intended to be good news for all who have joined with God to struggle against the evils of this world. To those who work for peace, the Second Coming is assurance that their labors are not in vain, and that one day peace will reign. To those who strive to eliminate poverty, the Second Coming means the day is coming when the hungry will be fed, the naked clothed, and the homeless housed. To those who strive to save the environment, the Second Coming is the promise and expectation that God will create a new heaven and a new earth, and that people will not hurt the earth any more.

The Second Coming affirms that all the good that is hoped for will be realized. Perhaps not soon, but inevitably.

McLaren Responds

Tony uses the language of lust and whores in this chapter—strong but biblical language, and I believe we need to let that strong language smack us, slam us, poke us, shake us. Any hybrid government-economy that promises security, prosperity, and identity has a lot of seductive power.

We Western Christians may be in bed with Babylon and not even realize it. What if our Christian subcultures, including many of our eschatologies, are perfectly designed to keep us slightly sedated as good consumers in Babylon? What if Babylon's nationalism and consumerism have neutered our gospel, declawed it, domesticated it, toned it down from a world-changing revolution to a soul-calming pacification? What if Marx was right about religion—our religion, Christianity—being an opiate, helping people become comfortable with injustice rather than enraged by it?

Our contemporary conservative eschatologies (like the currently popular Dispensational eschatology Tony describes in this chapter) strike me as desperate, escapist, and globally hopeless—eschatalogies of abandonment. *The world is going down the toilet, they say. There's no hope. It's all going to burn. So we should jump into the life rafts and paddle like mad away from from the sinking ship. We should retreat into our Christian enclaves, listen to Christian radio, watch Christian TV, pray, study the Bible, tell drivers what we believe with bumper stickers **in case of rapture, this vehicle will self-destruct**, keep our contact with the world at a minimum, concentrate on our personal righteousness, and anticipate heaven, a supernatural life* *beyond history*—instead of anticipating the just society that Tony calls "the goal of history."

Meanwhile, eschatologies that are more liberal and secular look toward education or technology or government or a vague principle of "the Progress of Western Civilization" to carry us toward that vision of a just society, with little concern for heaven and no expectation of (or need for) supernatural intervention. The just society will gradually emerge, it is thought, without apocalypse or cataclysm, through historical forces. And what are we to do to help the process along? Well, it would be nice to vote, we are told, and to try to be nice people. I'm all for being nice—but is the kingdom of God in the end a regime of niceness?

When I read the Bible, I see a mingling of both streams of prophecy. One stream plants in us a dream of a just and peaceful society on earth (as in heaven), a *hope* within our history. The other stream emphasizes an eternal destiny, a hope *beyond* history as we know it. One perspective calls us to whole-hearted action and sacrifice here and now, and the other reminds us that we must pray and trust, because God's kingdom does not come by might, or by power, but by the Spirit of the Lord.

I confess that I am still struggling to integrate these two streams. It would be so much easier to emphasize one and explain away the other. Perhaps one emphasis is the sperm and the other, the egg, each infertile on its own, but when merged with its opposite, a genesis occurs. This hybrid view opens up possibilities far better than either desperate abandonment or mere niceness. My hopes lie along this third path.

MISSING THE POINT:
the Bible

Brian D. McLaren

I love the Bible, and I want those I serve to learn to love the Bible, too. But sometimes I feel like a guy trying to hook up a buddy with a girl I know—you know, do a little matchmaking— but the introduction isn't going so well.

It's not because the two are incompatible, but how I set them up. I told my buddy that this girl was gorgeous, brilliant, outgoing, warm, accepting, personable, charming. "Perfect for you," I gushed.

Then they met. It's not that I stretched the truth about the girl—she's everything I said—but the truth is, she can be a bit shy at times. She doesn't just go around spilling her heart out to everyone. You have to know the right kinds of questions to ask her; until then, sometimes she can seem a little aloof. And although she is beautiful by anyone's standards, she dresses a little oddly by American standards, being from a Middle Eastern country and all. And I never mentioned her accent, and my buddy found her hard to understand, which made their first date awkward and uncomfortable.

I think they still have a chance, but next time I matchmake, I need to be more realistic.

That's how it is introducing the Bible in these strange and changing times. As we move from a world of high modernity to a transitional world, half in and half out of modernity and half into a new postmodern world that nobody quite knows how to describe—well, let's just say that introducing the Bible can be rocky.

Here is what I believe to be at the root of this rocky relationship between us and the Bible.

What the Bible Really Is

The Bible is an inspired gift from God—a unique collection of literary artifacts that together support the telling of an amazing and essential story. The artifacts include poetry, letters, short histories, and other genres that we don't have labels for. Even a familiar category like history needs to be used carefully, because we must avoid imposing modern biases and tastes on these ancient documents: they need to be taken and appreciated on their own terms.

The stories these artifacts support cover the amazing career of the descendents of a Middle Eastern nomad named Abraham. It traces their beginnings, growth, settlement, and resettlement through various social structures and economies, through many political arrangements, through good times and bad. This collection is uniquely profitable for teaching, rebuking, correcting, training, and equipping people so they can do good works for God.

What We (Mis)represented the Bible to Be

It's often the friends of the Bible who do it the most damage, as they entirely miss its purpose and message. Case in point: because modern Christians loved the Bible, they paid it four compliments, which have damaged as well as enhanced the Bible's reputation.

- *We compared the Bible to things we value highly.* Think encyclopedias (books with answers to everything), blueprints (how-to manuals), scientific formulae (universal laws), constitutions and annotated codes (rule books), and the like. In so doing we raised expectations; unfortunately, people expecting these things (answers to everything, a how-to manual, et cetera) are often disappointed, thus turning people away from the Bible.

- We claimed that the Bible was easy to understand, that any child could understand it. In some places that's probably true—but according to the Bible itself, at least some parts of it are very difficult to understand and easily misinterpreted (see 2 Peter 3:16, for example). Our sales pitch tried to commodify the Bible like other modern products—*It's easy! It's fast! It's convenient!*—and in so doing, we unintentionally sanctioned misunderstandings and bastard readings.

· *We presented the Bible as a repository of sacred propositions and abstractions.* Which was natural, for we were moderns—children of the 18th-century European Enlightenment—so we loved abstractions and propositions. Our sermons tended to exegete texts in such a way that stories, poetry, and biography (among other features of the Bible)—the "chaff"—were sifted out, while the "wheat" of doctrines and principles were saved. Modern Western people loved that approach; meanwhile, however, people of a more postmodern bent (who are more like *premodern* people in many ways) find the doctrines and principles as interesting as grass clippings.

· *We mass produced the Bible.* Thanks to technologies from the printing press to the Internet, you can find a copy of the Bible or hear Christian preaching just about anywhere, anytime now. Our mass production had benefits, of course—yet its ubiquity only reinforced the idea that the Bible is cheap and common. Furthermore, the Bible's ubiquity also fueled the perception that any individual may arrive at interpretations that are not only valid, but authoritative. This individualism transformed the Bible from the sacred text that gathers the community of faith into the ubiquitous text that divides through a multiplicity of divergent interpretations.

These misrepresentations were not malicious. But as we move from a western culture unified in the modern western mindset to a global culture with multiple perspectives sharing a more diverse postmodern mindset, it's time to take a fresh look at the Bible and debug our software of needless modern viruses. Otherwise people will reject the Bible needlessly—at least that's what they and we will *think* they're rejecting. What they're *actually* rejecting is the modern Western straitjacket in which we have corseted and even detained the Bible.

Those of us from theologically conservative backgrounds (that would include Fundamentalists, evangelicals, charismatics, and Pentecostals) are experts at identifying the modern liberal distortion of the Bible. To wit: liberals denied miracles, the supernatural in general, perhaps even God himself. So the Bible had to be expunged of all these primitive—that is, non-modern—elements, sanitized to fit the restricted and bland tastes of modernity. The Bible was put through the colander of Enlightenment modernity, and only what fit through the very small holes could be accepted: no pulp, no substance, just the filtered version of the Bible remained.

While we conservatives were decrying the modern liberal bias, we didn't realize we had developed our own modern *conservative* bias. We put Bible through a different colander. The result? Hardly anyone in conservative churches actually encounters the Bible any more. Instead, we read edited versions, annotated with commentary, sliced and diced and strained through a number of conservative filters— Dispensational, charismatic, Reformed, whatever. To understand a text usually means merely 1) finding the evidence that supports our preferred interpretation, and 2) reshaping, negating, or taming any biblical evidence that undermines our interpretation.

Perhaps more significant, we conservatives reflect the spirit of our modern age by redefining *hearing* or *reading* or *interpreting* as *analyzing*. Analysis, for premodern people, was one tool in the intellectual arsenal; for modern people, it has become the only tool.

Let me define analysis simply as breaking a whole down into its parts, as seeking understanding by reducing. To understand a car, we analyze it—take it apart, reduce it to a collection of rings, valves, pistons, and thingamajigs. To understand a cat, we dissect it into systems—nervous, digestive, reproductive, circulatory, et cetera.

Analysis, however, has two sides to it. Having broken anything down into its parts, we make some things clear, but other things less clear.

Take the car we took apart. Who owns it? What effect does it have on their social status? What role does it play in the global economy, or in the local environment? Having its parts laid out in front of us does not answer questions like these. Or the cat we dissected: who owned it? What was its personality like? What dogs did it torture? What cute and furry little kittens could it have given birth to if we hadn't killed it in order to analyze it, to "understand" it?

Similarly, when we theological conservatives seek to understand the Bible, we generally analyze it. We break it down into chapters, paragraphs, verses, sentences, clauses, phrases, words, prefixes, roots, suffixes, jots, and tittles. Now we understand it, we tell ourselves. Now we have conquered the text, captured the meaning, removed all mystery, stuffed it and preserved it for posterity, like a taxidermist with a deer head. But what have we missed? What have we lost by reduction?

For starters, by reducing the Bible to its parts, we forfeit the chance to ask holistic questions (as opposed to analytical questions). For example:

- Was this Bible book an example of a common Middle Eastern genre in its day?

- If so, how does it relate to other examples of the genre?

- Does this passage explore themes that are explored by other sacred texts from other religions?
  - What similarities and differences can be found?

- What were the cultural customs and standards of the day, and how does this story reflect them and perhaps violate them?

- How would it have felt to be each of the characters of the story?

- How does this whole book fit into the whole Bible?

- What themes does it share in common?

- What emphases are different and unique?

- Where do we see the unique personality of the writer coming through?

- Where do we see particular biases or literary devices or concerns of that specific time and place?

Instead of asking these kinds of holistic questions, we typically jump to the more familiar analytical questions:

- What do the Hebrew or Greek words in these sentences mean?

- What universal principles and accepted doctrines can we associate with this text (or can we use it to "prove" it)?

- How does this passage apply to our lives today?

These analytical questions, familiar to any theological conservative, speedily convert a biblical text into something supposedly useful to us—points for sermons, proofs for arguments, easy-application moral lessons for life. The less familiar holistic questions ask us to engage more deeply, patiently, and respectfully with the text—more like a lover of landscapes and less like a miner looking for a hill to strip-mine for a quick and saleable product.

Answering the less familiar questions involves different kinds of scholarship than we are used to, and requires of us little-used faculties—such as imagination and systems thinking.*

Aware, then, of how we tend to 1) inadvertently misrepresent the Bible, and 2) analyze it to a lethal degree—with this in mind, let me offer 10 suggestions for reclaiming the Bible for contemporary readers, so we won't miss the point.

Become Students, Seekers, Learners.

Get humble. The latest theories about virtue say that understanding is not just intellectual; it is also inextricably moral. Humble and curious people understand more than proud and lazy people. Intellectually flexible people discover more than rigid

---

*FOR EXAMPLE, APPLY THE TYPICAL ANALYTICAL QUESTIONS TO A STORY LIKE THE RAPE OF DINAH IN GENESIS 34, AND YOU'RE HARD-PRESSED TO COME UP WITH ANYTHING VERY USEFUL. YOU'RE LEFT WITH A DISTURBING STORY OF VIOLENCE, REVENGE, AND DECEIT. BUT IF YOU'RE MORE PATIENT, MORE OBSERVANT, LESS AGGRESSIVE WITH THE TEXT, LESS CONCERNED WITH MINING AN "APPLICATION"—THEN YOU MAY BEGIN TO NOTICE THAT THIS SECTION OF GENESIS FITS INTO A FASCINATING SYMMETRICAL STRUCTURE, IN WHICH THE STORY OF JACOB UNFOLDS IN A SERIES OF EPISODES, AND THEN THE STRUCTURE OF EPISODES SEEMS TO DOUBLE BACK ON ITSELF. WITHIN THIS STRUCTURE THE STORY OF DINAH'S RAPE PARALLELS THE STORY OF ISAAC AND ABIMELECH IN GENESIS 26—AND WHEN THE TWO STORIES ARE STUDIED IN COUNTER-POINT, ALL KINDS OF FASCINATING ISSUES BEGIN TO EMERGE. NOW THE TWO TEXTS BECOME A PROFOUND AND SOPHISTICATED ENGAGEMENT WITH THIS QUESTION: HOW DO THE JEWISH PEO-PLE RELATE TO THEIR NON-JEWISH NEIGHBORS, INCLUDING THE ISSUE OF INTERMARRIAGE? IN THE DINAH STORY VIOLENT AND AGGRESSIVE OPTIONS ARE EXPLORED; IN THE ABIMELECH STORY, MORE PEACEFUL AND COLLABORATIVE OPTIONS ARE EXPLORED. NOW THE STORIES YIELD NUANCED AND INTENSE ENGAGEMENTS WITH A COMMON QUESTION THAT CONCERNS RELIGIOUS COMMUNITIES TODAY.

ones. So we need to stop approaching the Bible only to confirm what we already think we know, and instead come at it like children, beginners—with a second innocence, as some interpreters call it.

Admit that Parts of the Bible Perplex, Bother, Confuse, or Concern You.
By taming the Bible—by fitting it neatly into our categories—we make the Bible safe but boring. The fact is, there are parts of the Bible that scandalize me. Not that this causes me to elevate my tastes and critique the text (like some theologically liberal readers), or to explain away the plain meaning of passages that describe the terrorist-style slaughter of women and children in the name of Jehovah (like a lot of theologically conservative readers). Instead, I simply acknowledge that a passage bugs me. And I can live with that. Maybe someday it will be resolved for me. Maybe not. That's okay.

Broaden Your Preoccupation with Propositions (What You Are Supposed to Think) So It Includes Mission (What You Are Supposed to Be and Do).
"We are embarked," as Blaise Pascal said. Because we cannot perfect our theory of navigation in a land-bound classroom, we must put to sea. It is only in sailing that we learn to sail. Similarly, we don't perfect our theology in a seminary or Sunday school course, whose textbook is the Bible. Our understanding of the Bible must be hammered out en route, at sea, in the nitty gritty of daily life.

So enough of trying to perfect our theory, hoping it will lead to a perfect practice. Instead we must learn by doing, intertwining theory with practice. This more

ancient (and contemporary) approach to learning means
that we won't expect to understand much more of the
Bible until we start doing what we already know. This
pushes us toward more missional readings of the Bible:
*What am I—and what are we—supposed to be doing in this world these
days, to fit in with God's creative and ongoing mission?* (as opposed
to propositional or doctrinal readings). That is the
urgent contemporary question. Sure, that requires
careful thinking, careful analysis, careful scholarship ...
but these intellectual pursuits are always in service of the
missional calling. They are undertaken on the voyage,
out at sea. In such a missional light, can you see how
absurd it is to think that we could get our theory right
first in a classroom, without living and serving and
loving and giving and suffering?

Give this missional approach a test drive. If you want
to read 1 Corinthians chapters 11–14 looking simply for
propositions about the role of women in the church,
you'll find them. The case is open and shut, with the
result that you'll require women to be silent in church.
But if you ask the more sophisticated question, *What is God
doing missionally in this passage?* the outcome is less clear, but
much more interesting (especially with 1 Corinthians
9:19ff as background). A missional reading of this
passage reveals that St. Paul is seeking to live out the
gospel in the framework of Corinthian culture—and this
requires the voluntary relinquishing of certain freedoms
in order to avoid cultural offense for the sake of the
gospel.

Taking the apostle's missional strategy seriously, and
not just mining for propositions, we might decide that
requiring women to be silent in church would be exactly

the *wrong* thing to do in a culture like ours, different as it is from Corinthian culture.

Drop Any Affair You May Have with Certainty, Proof, Argument—and Replace It with Dialogue, Conversation, Intrigue, and Search.
The ultimate Bible study or sermon in recent decades yielded clarity. That clarity, unfortunately, was often boring—and probably not that accurate, either, since reality is seldom clear, but usually fuzzy and mysterious; not black-and-white, but in living color.

So how about a Bible study or sermon that is successful not because everyone agrees on the preacher's interpretation, but because, when the sermon is over, everyone can't wait to talk about it and read and ponder and discuss it more, because they have become intrigued and mystified and enthralled? How about a congregation who may not have "captured the meaning" of the text, but a text that captured the imagination and curiosity of the congregation?

Drop Any Analytical-Reductionist Tendencies and Instead Focus on the Big Story, Always Moving Toward Your Place in Its Ongoing Trajectory.
Could you tell the Bible story in 15 minutes? Ten minutes? Five minutes? Two minutes? If not, you may not be ready to read the Bible, because each part is understandable only when we have the bigger picture that gives it context.

Without focusing on the Big Story, we are tempted to impose alien readings on the Bible. For example, if we reduce the Bible to an elaborate answer to the question, "How does a person go to heaven after he dies?"—if we think this is the Big Question the whole Bible is answering—we'll be prone to misunderstand major parts of the Bible that were written before that question was on anybody's mind (like the entire Old Testament). The Old Testament people were far more concerned about being the people of God *in* this life, not *after* this life. So when they performed sacrifices, for instance, they weren't seeking to get a clean slate so they could die forgiven as individuals and go to heaven after they died. To the contrary, they were seeking to remain pure enough as a community to participate in God's twofold promise to them: being blessed by God, and being a blessing to the whole world.

Find Things to Do with the Bible Other Than Read and Study It.
If you've never learned *lectio divina*—an ancient approach to Scripture cherished by the Benedictines—find someone who can teach it to you (or check out a book or a Web site).

Try an Ignatian reading, which requires you to imaginatively enter the story and seek to understand it from the inside instead of coolly analyzing it from a privileged distance.

Ever spend your Bible study time simply memorizing the Bible? (Just maybe an hour spent memorizing an entire passage—not just a verse, which is often taken out of its context—can occasionally be worth more than an hour spent listening to someone's monologue about the propositions he has extracted.)

Do a choral reading of a chapter of the Bible with a group—and do it several times, so it can be savored; then sit silently for 10 minutes to ponder and meditate on what you have read and heard together.

There are so many great things to do with the Bible other than study it. Remember: most Christians, through most of history, across most of the globe, were illiterate. Yet somehow they managed to love and serve God without ever once, in their entire lives, reading the Bible themselves.

Don't Try to Solve Mysteries—Seek and Revere Them.
Too many modern minds want to banish mystery, following the lead of modern science. But more and more scientists have realized that while they can develop models and labels for more and more phenomena, the depths of meaning and mystery in the cosmos will always exceed their grasp. When you feel that you have penetrated to an insight, go deeper, higher, farther— until you realize you are peering into a depth you cannot fathom. Don't be disappointed, but rather rejoice and revere not only the wonderful clarity revealed in Scripture, but also the amazing profundity hidden in Scripture.

Value Marginalized Readings and Readers.
The Bible was the book of the Jews and early Christians, who were nearly always marginalized, oppressed, and in danger. Privileged, comfortable, and secure people—like most of us—typically misunderstand the Bible because we cannot sufficiently identify with its original characters, writers, and readers. If you are privileged, find people who are not, and listen to their readings of Scripture. Value where their readings differ from yours and from each other, and expect new insight to spring from those differences.

Value dynamic tensions in the text itself. Some Old Testament texts, for instance, present the Israelite monarchy as a bad thing (by choosing a human king, the people conformed to their neighbors and rejected God as their king), while other texts celebrate the monarchy as a gift from God. Instead of trying to explain one or the other perspective away, why not say that the Bible presents an ambivalent view of the monarchy—that in some senses Israel's monarchy was a mistake; in other senses, a gift from God? After all, wouldn't you agree that all governments offer perils as well as benefits? That they fulfill God's purposes (as St. Paul affirms in Romans 13) *and* are capable of great damage (as all the "bad" kings of the Old Testament easily exemplify)?

And wouldn't oppressed people be most sensitive to the dangers as well as blessings of government?

Think of the Bible as a Book of Answers and Questions. What if the Bible is intended not merely to tell you what to think, but *how* to think—in the apostle Paul's words to Timothy, to make you "wise unto salvation"? In that case, the questions the Bible raises in your mind may be more important than the answers you find in it. Ever notice, when Jesus was asked a question, how often he answered with another question? What if God's answers to us are often questions? And what if, by inspiring questions in us, the Bible actually reads us, instead of us reading it? Remember what the book of Hebrews says, about the Bible penetrating deep within our hearts, reading our soul and spirit.

If You Preach, Preach Differently. Modern preaching is an acquired taste, and many churchgoers will be tempted to crucify you (or at least decrease their tithe to nine percent) if you depart from the conventions of modern homiletics. But some must

81

step out and boldly go where no preachers have gone before, into the unexplored territory of preaching in the new, emerging world.

Ironically, our style may become more like Jesus—even more like the Bible in general—as it becomes characterized by parable, story, conversation, proverb, poem, image, and surprise. All of which are a far cry from three points and an application, or "tell them what you'll tell them, tell them, and tell them what you told them," et cetera. If we're not careful, in fact, we may actually rekindle others' fascination with this wild and wonderful book called the Bible—and in the process rekindle our own fascination, too.

This is how I, at least, am trying to reclaim the Bible, this amazing collection of literary artifacts. And my growing passion inspires me to action—not just to study, study, study, but to live, serve, love, seek, find, rejoice, suffer, sacrifice, worship, invite, give, and receive. Which, I think, has been the point of the Bible all along.

Campolo Responds

I strongly affirm Brian's suggestion that we put ourselves in the place of Scripture writers. He points out correctly that, in general, the Bible was written by people who were poor and oppressed—and until we get into the mindset of such people, we don't understand its meaning.

Brian is quite right when he tells us that the Bible should not be considered a mere repository of propositional truths. But certainly we must be aware of those sections of the Bible that *do* contain propositional truths, and of the importance of analyzing those doctrines—for they have ultimate significance for the Christian faith. Most biblical scholars would contend that the apostle Paul's theological propositions have largely defined traditional Christianity.

Also, Brian may have bought into postmodern thinking just a little bit too much for me. As I see it, Jacques Derrida, the famous postmodern deconstructionist philosopher, and his followers contend that the text of Scripture has no single interpretation; instead the Bible should be read as though it was a Rorschach test. They tell us to see in the text whatever meaning we want to impose on it. They tell us that no single interpretation should be considered objectively valid. The text, say these postmodernists, has a life of its own—and once it is written, the reader provides the meaning. To me, that approach to the Bible has inherent dangers.

WORLD

MISSING THE POINT:
Evangelism

Brian D. McLaren

You walk into the office and your buddy is doing his best imitation of a televangelist—strutting, gesticulating, laying his hands on people, yelling "Amen! Amen!" Your coworkers are howling. Until they see you, that is. Everyone stops laughing; they're obviously embarrassed. "We better end the show here, folks," someone says awkwardly. "We don't want to offend our resident saint." The group disperses before you can say, "Hey, I didn't mean to spoil the fun."

Your buddy says, "Yeah, bad timing...I didn't even get to take the collection..." But then he turns and looks at you. "Do you really believe all that Christianity stuff?" he asks.

And there it is: an opening to share your faith. You want your friend to know that yes, you do believe, but no, you don't buy all that late-night TV preacher stuff—the geometric hairdos, the manipulative financial appeals, the gaudy spectacles, the inflated claims, the cartoonish emotionalism. You want to tell him that your faith has substance, that it makes sense, that it's made a difference in your life—and that it could do the same for him, too. How do you give a good answer to an honest question like his?

The art of giving reasonable answers to questions about our faith is called *apologetics*. If you're like most of us, you are in touch every day with people who are skeptical or curious about your faith, and so you are exactly the kind of person who would benefit from a crash course in apologetics.

But apologetics isn't just about helping skeptics. Even the most committed of believers face doubts and questions of their own, and they need honest, reasonable answers too. So apologetics isn't the exclusive province of esoteric eggheads and nerdly know-it-alls. Neither is it just for pastors and missionaries. *Everybody* needs a dose of apologetics.

This is because the cost of sloppy apologetics is high. Without clear and convincing answers to common questions about the faith, believers lack confidence. They're quicker to abandon their faith and slower to share it with others. Their children often inherit a sort of bad faith, a faith that squints its mind and tries not to think. And meanwhile, without good apologetics, millions of spiritual seekers wander somewhere south of good faith.

Take my friend Steve. He's a scientist and an atheist. As a teenager, he told me, he was a sincere churchgoer and the president of his church youth group. And then came the day when his Sunday school teacher said, "You have a choice to make. Either you will believe in evolution or you will believe in God. It's one or the other—science or faith." Steve was intrigued with biology, and when he went away to college and studied science, he followed his Sunday school teacher's dictum and left his faith behind. That was a case of bad apologetics.

Another friend, Gary, is a surgeon. He's a fine person, active in the community, a dedicated father and husband, a fun friend, and—like Steve—an atheist. I asked him about his religious orientation (or lack thereof), and his story was similar. As a boy he attended church every Sunday and a religious school Mondays through Fridays. A curious kid, he asked a lot of questions about God, church, sin, life. Whatever his question, his parents, teachers, and clergy gave him the same answer again and again: "Don't ask questions. Just believe." Another case of bad apologetics with sad consequences.

What are the most common questions that people like Gary ask? I have found that they are apologetic questions, and they tend to fall in five broad categories.

Questions about the existence of God

These include questions about whether science alone can

account for the universe…why evil and suffering can exist if there is a good and all-powerful God…why, if God does exist, there are so many religions with so many competing and contradictory claims about God.

Effective responses to questions like these avoid getting bogged down in peripheral issues—so stay away from arguments about the age of the earth, evolution, et cetera. Effective answers tend to focus on a few key questions:

- Can the universe with all its mystery, order, complexity, life, and wonder—including the expansive world of human experience and values—be explained satisfactorily by mechanistic time plus chance plus nothing?

- Now that science generally agrees that there is a genesis point—such as the Big Bang—does it make more sense than ever to believe that there is a creator?

- If there is no God, is it possible to imagine any real basis for values like justice, compassion, beauty, goodness, and truth?

- Are the spiritual longings of humanity merely an evolutionary fluke, or could the longings themselves be evidence for a spiritual dimension to reality—i.e. God?

- Can the problem of evil be solved satisfactorily if there is no God?

- To questions about the multiplicity of religions: what is the realistic alternative? What else might one expect, given human curiosity and spiritual hunger, combined with our limitations and mixed motives?

Questions about How God Reveals Himself

These include questions about—

- The Bible

- The claims we Christians often make about the Bible (which are often more problematic than anything the Bible says about itself)
- Apparent discrepancies within the Bible or between the Bible and science
- The historicity of biblical stories (especially miracles)
- Whether various world religions contain equally valid revelations from God, and can therefore be reconciled
- The existence of absolute truth (by which people often actually mean *absolute knowledge* or *undoubtable certainty*)

Effective responses to these kinds of questions treat the Bible less as a catalogue of inspired abstractions, and more as a record of people who had authentic spiritual experiences with God. Good apologists, furthermore, realize that what really matters to most spiritual seekers these days is not intellectual certainty, but honest faith. They are more responsive to the Bible as a book intended to inspire their faith than as a scientific textbook.

Questions about the Behavior of Religious People

Why are there so many hypocrites? Why is so much evil done in the name of religion? Why did my friend become such an arrogant, judgmental, and unlikable person after she became born again? Why are Christians so intolerant of homosexuals?

If you want to respond effectively to these kinds of questions, you are usually wise to begin by acknowledging the wrongs that are so common among the religious. Rather than defending the indefensible, your own humility becomes an apologetic. Sometimes the best apologetic is simply to apologize: "Yes, I'm so sorry...sometimes people do horrible things in the name of God. It's tragic. You're right."

Then ask people what alternative there might be. Is it realistic that God make everyone instantly perfect upon their conversion, to protect his reputation from their inevitable failures? Sometimes I point out that even if one bad apple spoiled the whole barrel (which is nearly impossible, but assuming it did), a whole barrel-full of bad apples doesn't ruin the tree. I affirm a person's disgust with hypocrisy, and say something like, "When you make a faith commitment yourself, you'll want to be sure to avoid those mistakes, right? You'll want to be genuine, authentic, honest, and not pushy—which is exactly what God wants you to be too, I believe."

Questions about Specific Christian Beliefs and Practices

These include beliefs such as the deity and uniqueness of Christ, sexual morality, heaven and hell, et cetera.

These questions are usually raised when people are getting closer to making a faith commitment, which means your responses need to build on whatever amount or depth of faith they already have. For example, you might say, "Since you're already comfortable praying to God, why don't you ask God to help you understand this?" This way they exercise what faith they have, which is the best way to build more faith.

I also take advantage of the diversity of opinion among Christians. If people ask me about the Christian doctrine of hell, I often say, "Well, Christians have three different approaches to the subject of hell." If they ask about the deity of Christ, I mention that Christians in the first centuries of the faith struggled to articulately and accurately describe Jesus' identity, because he didn't fit easily in any existing categories. If they ask about the trinity, I make it clear that the trinity is an attempt to protect us from making false statements about God the Father, Jesus, and the Holy Spirit; the doctrine is far from a mathematical equation that in any way defines the being of

God, which is (and obviously must be) *way* beyond the comprehension of our puny three-pound brains.

These kinds of responses appeal to individuals who are turned off not by Christian doctrine, but by the glib and easy way in which many Christians articulate it—as if there were no difficulties, no controversies, no mysteries.

Practical questions about how to know God

These include how to get closer to God, how to experience God, how to know God's will, how to deal with life's problems from a godly perspective, et cetera.

When people ask these kinds of questions, they're often reacting to inaccurate or unbalanced sermons or books or careless preachers. So it can help to ask them what they're afraid of, or what they want to avoid—and we can often help them articulate their *real* question beneath the *apparent* question.

A friend asks you, for instance, how she can know the will of God. A little probing, however, reveals her fear that if she becomes a Christian, God will make her into some sort of freak—at which point you can assure her that God only wants to make her into a work of art, someone whose character reflects the beauty and dignity of Jesus Christ. Definitely *not* a cheesy, religious weirdo.

Let's say that you aimed at becoming a better apologist over the next five or ten years. Good for you! So plan to spend some time living in these five kinds of questions. Read books, consult trusted and thoughtful teachers, dialogue with friends. Pray, too, asking God to help you learn so you can help others learn. In the course of a few years, you will develop more depth in your understanding of your faith—and that increased depth will make your faith more valuable to you, as it makes you more of a resource to others.

But don't stop there. As apologetics is changing—as we move from a modern, familiar environment to a new, less familiar one—our apologetic also needs to change. Modernity constrained us to operate in a rationalistic framework—that is, based on reason alone—and our apologetic accordingly focused on logic, evidence, proof, answers, scholarship, reasons, arguments, and appeals to authority.

As we move into the emerging culture, however, our apologetic will focus more and more on beauty, goodness, experience, questions, mystery, community, and humility.

Some examples of what I mean:

• In the recent past we argued about evolution versus faith. In the emerging culture, we may say, "Let's assume evolution is true, or partially true. Is it possible that evolution itself could be a creation of God, a process which God would create in order to create new life forms?"

• In the recent past we generally began our apologetic by arguing for the Bible's authority, then used the Bible to prove our other points. In the future we'll present the Bible less like evidence in a court case and more like works of art in an art gallery. The Bible will become valuable not for what it proves, but for what it reveals.

• In the recent past we attempted to explain how evil and suffering can exist in a world created by a good and all-powerful God. In the future we'll return the question to the questioner, maybe something like this: "If you don't believe in God, then how do you explain evil and suffering—and what meaning or hope can you find in all the injustice?" Or "You're right: evil is intolerable. It shouldn't exist. There's no good reason for it, nor can there be. Which is exactly why Christians dedicate ourselves to overcoming it with good."

93

- In the recent past we talked a lot about absolute truth, attempting to prove abstract propositions about God (for instance, proving the sovereignty of God). In the emerging culture, however, we will be much more interested in *embodied truth* (for instance, how Jesus demonstrated God's mercy), and we will want to convey real-life stories about God—stories from our lives as well as from the Bible.

- In the recent past we assumed people would come to faith in a linear way, moving along a predictable path, as isolated individuals. In the future we'll expect people to spiral in on faith, to approach it from many angles at once, and to discover it in community rather than individually. We may well see the process of coming to faith as a wonderful integration of intellect and emotion, experience and reflection, privacy and community, mystery and clarity.

In many ways apologetics today is like selling gasoline during the '70s—you needed to provide both leaded and unleaded gas. Or it's like music in the '90s—you needed to sell both cassettes as well as CDs. To be a good apologist today, you need to offer both standard and innovative responses to common questions.

As cultures change, as new questions arise, we get to keep growing in our understanding of the faith and in our ability to make it clear to others. Which is really just following Jesus' example, who took God's message and translated it into a form that people could understand—in word, deed, and example.

Word, deed, and example: it's important to keep these three integrated. After all, Jesus never said that the world would be convinced of the truth about him solely based on our logical words. Along with wise and true words, our good deeds, he said, would lead people to glorify God with us, and the living example of our loving relationships would be the ultimate evidence that he is real. Put good deeds and living examples of loving relationships together with clear and honest words, and you'll have the best apologetic of all.

I've wondered how my spiritually seeking friends would advise me about my apologetics—what those who are not yet Christians would say would be more helpful to them. I think they'd say something like this:

- *Build a relationship.* When people ask questions about matters of ultimate concern, they are seldom looking for mere answers. They're looking for a mentor. So avoid slipping into Answer Man mode. Instead let your friend's questions open the door for dialogue: you ask questions, listen to your friend's thoughts, share your own experiences, and demonstrate genuine love and concern. Jesus commonly turned a question into a conversation by answering questions with questions. You too may find that the best response to many questions is this question: *Why is that question important to you?* If I understand what's *behind* the question, I'm more likely to respond to my friend's need instead of just her words.

- *Don't offer a cheap or easy answer for a deep, complex question.* Quoting a Bible verse may be very convincing for you— but if your friend doesn't acknowledge the Bible as an authoritative or trustworthy text, quoting a verse to him will probably seem like a way of brushing off his question.

- *Feel free to say you don't know.* Nobody expects you to have all the answers—unless you pretend to. Your friend would rather have you take the posture of a humble fellow seeker, someone who has unanswered questions of his own, rather than a know-it-all. Pretending to know more than you do does not enhance your claim to hold an honest and true faith.

- *Rely on the power of stories.* Your stories—about how you came to faith, about how God has made a difference in your life—are important data for a questioning friend. Think of Paul in the book of Acts—he's constantly telling his own story. But don't stop with your own story: tell biblical stories, too. Jesus seldom taught without telling a parable.

- *Keep the conversation going.* After you've given your friend your best answers, find out if they helped. Ask, "Does that make sense? Does that help?" If the answer is no, keep the conversation going. In fact, keep the conversation going even if the answer is yes!

- *Encourage your friends to exercise whatever faith they have.* For example, I often say something like this to people: "If you were about to enter a dark room, and wanted to find out if anyone was there, you'd call out, *Hey! Is anybody in there?* I think you can do the same with God. You can say, *God, if you're there, please help me to find you. I am reaching out to you. I don't have a lot of faith, but I have enough to at least reach out and ask for your help and guidance in my search.*" Similarly, I often encourage people to start reading the Bible or attending church, even if they don't believe yet—just to nourish the little faith they do have.

- *If some questions are beyond you, then introduce your friend to others who can understand, relate, and help.* Apologetics is ultimately a team endeavor, so it only makes sense to make your relational network available to your questioning friend. Similarly, pass on to friends resources that have helped you.

- *Don't assume there's only one right way to answer a question.* To the difficult question "Why does God allow pain and suffering in the world?" there are dozens of responses, some more helpful than others. A single answer may leave a seeker cold—but three or four responses, taken together, will help the person.

- *Be sensitive to God's Spirit at work in the situation.* The ancient prophet Jeremiah passed on a wonderful promise from God: that those who seek will surely find, if they seek with all their heart. Jesus echoed the promise, and said that his Spirit would be sent to guide people into truth. So I try to remember that I'm here simply to fit in with God's initiatives toward this person, whom he loves far more than I ever can.

- *Don't pressure or rush anyone to believe.* Jesus didn't. In fact, he made it easy for people to walk away. And not because he didn't care, but because he knew that people must be fully persuaded in their own minds and hearts. Rushed conversions are as dangerous as premature births.

- *Always be respectful and gentle with spiritual questioners.* Peter wrote to "always be ready to give an answer to those who ask you the reason for the hope that is in you. And do so with gentleness and respect" (I Peter 3:15). If you are defensive—if you fail to respond to your questioner kindly and patiently—it doesn't matter what you say: your apologetic has already failed.

  Furthermore, being respectful means you don't insult or mock other people's religions, cultures, or beliefs—no matter how wrong or incomplete you believe them to be. Paul exemplified this respectful approach at a place in Athens called Mars Hill—one of the best examples of an effective apologetic anywhere. Read about it in Acts 17.

- *Educate yourself on the most common apologetic questions.* There are only so many hot issues, so prepare a half dozen really good responses to them.

You're not going to argue anyone into faith. In fact, being argumentative will probably drive questioners away from faith— at least from *your* kind of faith. Pushing someone into believing what they don't want to believe is missing the point. On the other hand, become their friend, their conversation partner, their spiritual consultant, their servant—that's better for them, for you, for the kingdom.

Campolo Responds

What Brian hints at and suggests throughout this clear and helpful chapter, I wish he would just out and say it: the best apologetic is a personal testimony. When you tell someone what Jesus means to you, and how Jesus has affected your life, that is probably taken more seriously than any intellectual argument that can be offered. And, appropriately, my defense of this belief lies not in argument, but in two stories.

While teaching at the University of Pennsylvania, my advisees included a brilliant, articulate neo-Marxist-atheist, and his friend—a committed Christian, but by no means an intellectual.

I was a bit dismayed when I heard that not only were the two of them going off to Cornell for graduate work, but that they would be roommates. The neo-Marxist loved to argue, I knew, and he was formidable and convincing. I feared that the less intellectually competent Christian friend would be gradually be overwhelmed.

You can imagine my surprise a year and a half later when I visited with them both at Cornell and discovered that the neo-Marxist had become a Christian. How was that possible, I asked, seeing what a good arguer he was?

"I always won the arguments," the ex-atheist said. "It seemed like every evening I would give him an array of good reasons why religion in general was ludicrous, and how the belief that Jesus was the incarnation of God was untenable. But at the end of every argument, after I had won the confrontation decisively, my buddy would always say, 'But I know that Jesus is real. I know that Christ is alive. I sense his presence. I have experienced a sense of his leading in my life. You may have won the arguments, but you cannot undo what I know to be true. Jesus is alive in me.'

"What could I say to that? Sooner or later my attacks were no match for his defense. How could I unconvince him of something so obviously real in his life?"

Story two. Having concluded my sociology of religion lecture at Dartmouth College, a student came to the front of the hall to ask me how I could be so naïve as to believe in God and in the Bible.

"I decided to," I replied. "Having once made that decision, I have continued to build intellectual supports for what I had already decided was true." My apologetic, I explained, was determined by an *a priori* commitment. I believed first, then constructed arguments to support what I believed.

My candidness in admitting that my faith depended on an existentialist decision rather than on rational argument gave me the freedom to ask him a question.

"Why do you *not* believe in God and in the Bible? Isn't it true that somewhere along the line you decided *not* to believe? And having made that decision, didn't you construct arguments to support your *a priori* decision?

"In the end, isn't what we believe more highly contingent upon decisions we make rather than on empirical evidence?"

He saw my point, and we agreed to disagree about God and the Bible. But at least we both avoided the idea that being a Christian believer is less intellectually credible than being a non-believer.

I believe that in the game of apologetics, the best defense is a good offense. We need to demonstrate that non-belief is as much a faith commitment as belief.

MISSING THE POINT: Social Action

Tony Campolo

To most evangelicals, "social action" as a theological tenet once had liberal, suspicious, and unbiblical connotations. Such "social gospelers" were considered politically left, semi-Christians who had forsaken a biblically based salvation message for a diluted gospel of mere social ethics. And because it was largely the theological liberals who embraced social action, evangelicals reacted by making both liberals and social action their adversaries.

No longer. Over the past few decades, evangelicals have increasingly talked about a holistic gospel that incorporates in its salvation story a Jesus who came into the world to minister to all needs of a hurting humanity—physical and social needs as well as spiritual needs.

Evangelical theologians like Carl Henry (founder of *Christianity Today* and Ron Sider (founder of Evangelicals for Social Action) were among the first to begin helping evangelicals see what their uneasy consciences had always known the Scriptures taught. Today staunchly evangelical organizations like Promise Keepers have made racial reconciliation a primary emphasis of their efforts. Even some fundamentalist churches now readily claim that caring for the poor and standing up for justice for the oppressed is part of their mission.

These days most evangelical church members will chip in willingly when the youth group raises airfare for a trip to build houses for poor Latin Americans who live in shacks. No one raises an eyebrow when the youth group collects blankets for the homeless. They will sponsor their church's teenagers in a "hunger walk." Sure, they may want assurances that the salvation story gets told in the process, and that the poor or the hungry get a chance to make commitments to Christ. Some still think that social action is valuable only to the degree that it effects spiritual conversions. But even with such mixed motives, most church groups—regardless of their theological persuasion—are in direct, face-to-face ministry to the poor in some way or another.

Furthermore, it's become obvious that such ministry transforms the servers probably more than it does the served. Some youth ministries, in fact, are organized wholly around successive short-term mission trips. "Those trips do more to change our youth into real Christians than anything else we ever did," one youth minister said. And part of the rationale behind similar programs at Eastern University—which serve needy children in Philadelphia as well as impoverished peoples in third-world countries—is that such involvement with the poor has a transforming influence on the students. Students who have been so transformed are much more likely to give their lives to missionary vocations.

But is it enough to relieve their poverty for a season? To meet the summer needs of a poor family, but then to leave them to the poverty that inevitably returns shortly after the youth group goes home to September classes and Halloween parties and Christmas celebrations?

What can be done to eliminate poverty, rather than to merely relieve it for a season? Can we, like the adage says, not merely give starving families fish to eat now and then, but actually teach them how to fish so that they can feed themselves?

A common Christian response to this is to support education programs that train the poor in skills that will enable them to make a living. In answer to this question, missionary societies have founded training programs and schools around the world, with the express purpose of helping the poor out of their desperate situations. The goal is to deliver the poor from their poverty for not just a day or a week—but for the rest of their lives.

To this end Christian missions are now actually developing small businesses and cottage industries that the poor can own and run themselves. Take the Illinois-based Opportunity International, for instance. In only a decade this organization has used micro-loans to create more than a million jobs in third-world countries. When you consider that a third-world family averages six persons, you realize that this means that six million people are delivered from poverty on an ongoing basis.

I was part of such a micro-enterprise in the Dominican Republic. In an impoverished neighborhood in Santo Domingo, we started a tiny factory that produced sandals made out of worn-out automobile tires. We told the younger children that we would pay them fifty cents for each junked tire they brought us from the city's trash dumps and vacant lots. (It was when we started getting a lot of *new* automobile tires that we knew it was time to make some adjustments!) With simple tools and very little training, it was possible for young people to cut out sandals from discarded tires and fashion them into attractive and durable footwear. The boys would then take the sandals out onto the streets of the city and sell them—in this way providing an income for their families.

All of this is to say that, when we talk about Jesus, we must make it clear that he is not just interested in our well-being in the afterlife. He is a Savior who is at work in the world today trying to save the world from what it is, and make it into a place where people can live together with dignity.

Religiously sponsored endeavors like this have become so successful, in fact—have done more good with less money than, say, similar government-sponsored programs—that the federal government has of late become very interested in such faith-based programs. Especially during the Clinton and Bush Two administrations, people in Washington have been trying to figure out ways to funnel federal dollars into faith-based programs, hoping that such a partnership with religious communities can better address the needs of the poor.

Yet I have some concerns about religious groups getting into bed with the government, not the least of which is the constitutional need for separation of church and state. Furthermore, I am convinced that the reason that faith-based programs are so successful is exactly because they are faith-based and *not* government sanctioned. It is the spiritual dimension of these programs that makes them work so well.

The best example of what I'm talking about can be found in the work of Teen Challenge, a Pentecostal ministry to young drug addicts that is based on the belief that the filling with the Holy Spirit is central to a user's deliverance from addiction. While most rehab programs have about a 10-percent success rate, Teen Challenge's reaches about 80 percent. Obviously, to remove the spiritual dimensions of Teen Challenge would be to kill its success. Yet if Teen Challenge were to seek recognition by and funding from the federal government, that organization could conceivably be pressured to minimize what the government could call "proselytizing" activities—despite the fact that those activities are exactly what makes Teen Challenge so successful.

I am worried that many Christian ministries to the needy will eventually take federal dollars and gradually become dependent on government funding. Then, if the courts eventually require it—and many legal experts contend that they eventually will—these ministries will have to abandon their religious emphasis in order to continue their operations. What the government giveth, the government can take away—and I am concerned that these agencies, which are expanding their operations with federal dollars, will have to give up their spiritual cutting edge just to keep getting the money they need to stay in business.

"Connecting government with faith-based programs is a lot like mixing ice cream with horse manure," one American mayor has observed. "It won't hurt the manure, but it will really mess up the ice cream."

When you minister to the poor of the world directly and individually, even governments may lend you a hand. But begin suggesting that a government's political and economic systems actually *create* privation and suffering, and you will be told that you're in over your head—that you're messing around in areas that Christians ought to leave alone

"When I gave them food, they called me a saint," said Bishop Donn Helder Camaro of Recife, Brazil. "Yet when I asked why they had no food in the first place, they called me a communist." Ask questions like that, and many in government are convinced you've stopped preaching and gone to meddling. If like a good Samaritan you dress the wounds of a mugged man who had been left for dead, you are deemed a godly person. But if the muggings continue, and you ask why the government doesn't have police patrols and better lighting along the road, you will be asked if you, as a religious leader, have overstepped your bounds.

It only complicates things that those who have vested interests in sustaining the political-economic system are, ironically, high-profile or active church members. Look at campaign finance reform in the U.S.—those who oppose reform are leaders in the tobacco industry, those who hold controlling interests in oil companies. For the existing system of campaign financing lets them wield huge influence in Congress to protect their tobacco or oil interests. And, because they are often faithful church attenders, they would argue that the Bill of Rights requires that church leaders stay out of government affairs.

What they fail to realize is that the Bill of Rights stipulates separation of church and state precisely so churches would be free from state domination and thus be able to speak to the state with a prophetic voice. All through the Hebrew Bible, prophets of God dared to speak up in governmental contexts for the poor and the oppressed, and called on their rulers to treat them with justice. Jesus himself was in this prophetic tradition: he started his ministry by declaring that the kingdom of God was at hand (Mark 1:14-15), and that this Kingdom would be good news for the poor (Luke 4:18).

You will incur the deepest suspicion, however—at least in the U.S.—if you have the audacity to question the capitalistic system itself. Capitalism is a divinely ordained economic system, say many Americans, and any who question capitalism are the enemies of God.

Yet how can capitalism be divinely ordained when its most revered theorist, Adam Smith, writes in *The Wealth of Nations* that greed is what makes capitalism work? "It is not from the benevolence of the butcher, the brewer, or the baker that we expect our dinner, but from their regard to self-interest. We address ourselves, not to their humanity, but to their self love." What religion regards as foul, capitalism pronounces as good. It is from the "luxury and the caprice of the rich man" and from "his natural selfishness and rapacity" that society advances, Smith believed.

When those who wield economic power are out of control, and serve their own interests to the detriment of the masses, the poor, and the powerless, Christians must speak prophetically and pronounce God's judgment against such destructive self-interest.

You never know when a prophetic message will bring voluntary compliance with what is right. More than two decades ago, some of my students at Eastern College conducted research that addressed the question, *How could a small group of Christians effect micro-social changes in society?* For answers to that question, they designed a plan that sought to bring social justice to the Dominican Republic—a small country that needed justice in a big way.

"If this is really such a workable plan," a student said one day, "why don't we enact it? Why don't we see what we can do about changing the Dominican Republic?"

The first step of this "Christian revolutionary movement" was to buy stock in Gulf & Western, a large multinational corporations that we believed dominated the economy of the Dominican Republic. It owned hotels, resorts, massive tracts of real estate, and the major sugar producer.

Each student bought one share of stock in Gulf & Western— an act that entitled them to attend the stockholders' meeting. During the meeting, the students took turns reading from the Bible and calling Gulf & Western to economic responsibility. We asked them to raise the pitifully low wages of their sugar workers. We pointed out that the corporation had led the nation to gradually depend on a single-crop economy. We complained about the failure of the corporation to provide education and medical services for the people in the region of D.R. that they dominated.

The students expected to be laughed out of the meeting— which would set them up for the next stage: confrontation, which could become ugly.

Instead, the corporate executives of Gulf & Western actually listened. A series of negotiations took place over the next several months—and not only with us, but with other organizations that were also committed to improving the economic and social life of the people of the Dominican Republic.

And it actually happened: Gulf & Western went public with a plan to help the people of D.R. The corporation committed itself to working with Mt. Sinai Medical Center of New York to create health services in the communities throughout the eastern half of the nation...it committed itself to testing the soil, so that land that *could* produce food for the indigenous corporate population would be reserved for that purpose...it committed itself to an array of educational programs that included a new university to train teachers, lawyers, nurses, and engineers.

The students were stunned. And amazingly enough, Gulf & Western followed through on their promises: they spent a half billion dollars on these programs over the next five years, and in the process brought about radical change in the lives of the people of that region.

Not all episodes have such happy endings. Standing up for justice can land you in jail, or worse. Martin Luther King, Jr. is recognized today by most Americans as a great moral leader who stirred the consciousness of America. But if you lived during the civil rights movement in the 1950s and '60s, you'll remember how sheriffs and mayors and governors put him behind bars. We may revere King now, but his practice of civil disobedience then earned him condemnation from pulpits as a Marxist.

Imprisonment and violence are not the only consequences of working as a Christian for social justice. There is the danger of short-circuiting your pursuit of social justice by aligning yourself with a political party. It is unfortunate, and serves to divide rather than improve things, that denominational leaders within the National Council of Churches are likely to align politically with Democratic Party, or that most members of evangelical and fundamentalist churches (with the exception of African-American congregations) are likely to identify with the

GOP. In such an atmosphere it's difficult to remember that Jesus is neither a Democrat nor a Republican. When I am asked to which party I belong, I say, "Cite the issue." On some issues I'm with one party, on other issues I'm with the other party.

Sojourners editor Jim Wallis has tried to create a coalition of Christians from across the political spectrum to work on behalf of the poor. The old dichotomy, he has declared, separated left from right, Democrat from Republican. Wallis calls for a new kind of politics that demands the concern of Christians for those the Bible calls "the least of these." No child should be without a decent education, a balanced diet, and proper health care, he declares. Leave No Child Behind—a movement that is uniting Christians with divergent political points of view—just may be marking an important transition in American Christian social action.

Of all the "the principalities and powers" that St. Paul writes of in Ephesians 6:12, the government is one of those entities against which we are to wrestle as we seek to see God's will "done on earth, as it is in heaven." Not that this wrestling is always clear: when do we fight, and when do we submit (Romans 13:5, 1 Peter 2:13ff)? Therefore we must always deal with these principalities and powers and governments with fear and trembling, for political decisions seldom lend themselves to simple answers. When you struggle with government policies, you are likely to find yourself in controversy, and taking stands marked more by moral ambiguities than by stark right and wrong sides.

Social action is no longer just an option for thinking Christians. The only questions remaining for us are what issues will we address, what will we say, and then what will we do?

Tony's last question sticks in my mind like a burr on my pant leg: *What issues should matter most to us?*

Two issues seem to be at the top of the list for many of my Christian friends: ending abortion (by making it illegal?) and doing something about homosexuals (by outlawing them? Jailing them? Shaming them? Asking them to leave the premises?). No doubt, our culture is in a sexually manic episode, and we need to return to sexual sanity. But in the big scheme of things, other issues rise to the top of my list when I think, pray, look around, read the papers, travel, listen, look.

Overpopulation. True, Adam and Eve were told to be fruitful and multiply, but this may be the one biblical command humans have obeyed pretty well. How much multiplying is enough, and how many is too many? Six billion? 12 billion? 24 billion? 48 billion? Neither can the question be answered in only global terms: it has to be addressed regionally, too. If you have more people than a region can support, an avalanche of other problems will follow (such as the others in my list here).

Consumerism. Take the country of China, whose population is currently nearing 1.3 billion. Let's imagine that China succeeds in achieving a zero-percent growth rate, and then focuses on raising the standard of living of its people. Let's imagine that the average Chinese person, as his standard of living increases, wants to consume an additional one-quarter pound of pork a year for the next five years.

Hardly noticeable, right? Well, maybe not: that quarter of a pound of pork per person per year means that China will demand more than

300 million more pounds of pork per year. Now figure in how much corn is needed to produce that much pork...then how much manure is produced by that many pigs...then the impact on global commodities markets by this increased demand for corn...then the amount of polluted water produced by runoff from these pig farms.

Now make that annual quarter-pound increase a *monthly* increase...and broaden the demand from pork to fish, plastic, paper, oil, electricity, lumber, clean drinking water...and then add India into the equation.

You get the point. Even without population growth—if the whole world aims to consume resources at even a fraction of the rate Americans do, the world is in deep trouble. Jesus' words, "A person's life does not consist in the abundance of possessions"—or consumables—now seem less like limitation and more like salvation.

Ecology. Rising human populations, rising consumer demands, and the pollution produced by human consumption—these all conspire to stretch our planet's capacity for self-renewal beyond its limits in terms of air and water quality, topsoil and rainforest maintenance, and temperature regulation. And limits broken in one area can cascade into others, creating an environmental avalanche of apocalyptic proportions.

Meanwhile, if God wants to check in with us on how we've done as stewards of God's planet, we have fewer and fewer extant species to report each year.

Genetic engineering and psychopharmacology. Will human beings take control of their own evolution in the coming century? What will that mean? Is the power of DNA greater than the power of nuclear weapons—and if so, how will we deal with the greatest power we have ever wielded? What does God want us to do with that power? What are just and unjust or wise and unwise uses of it?

Meanwhile, as we discover more about brain chemistry, we face another realm of ethical questions as Christians. For example, if you could take a happy pill that makes you more kind, loving, generous, joyful, and trusting, and less self-absorbed, grouchy, dark, and uptight—should you? Should a young single man take an anti-Viagra pill while he's single and hormonally charged? Does that make him more chaste? If we could take a pill that would increase our concentration or our IQs by 40 percent, should we? Which ones of us should get the pill first? Politicians? Military strategists? Marketing reps? Seminary professors?

Racial, religious, and ethnic hatred. Will a few desperate militant Muslims force a global showdown, issuing a convert-or-die ultimatum backed up not with swords, but with genetically engineered viruses or dirty nuclear bombs? Will the poorest countries of the world grow jealous of U.S. prosperity (and global domination to preserve it), and band together in hatred against Americans? Will tribal hatred in Africa unleash more holocausts? Will the church have anything to say about loving enemies, when that message of Jesus seems at once naïve and necessary?

Poverty. Will the staggering gap between the rich and the poor widen more? Will that inequity fuel the hatreds mentioned above? If global capitalism makes the rich richer and leaves the poor in poverty, what will we do? Merely thank God we're among the rich?

Can we say we love God if we don't love our neighbor who lives in an overpopulated, underfed, overpolluted, undermedicated, strife-torn slum?

MISSING THE POINT:
Culture

Brian D. McLaren

Despite our sincerity and best of motives, preachers like me mess people up. It's unintentional, believe me: we're just trying to protect people. But we damage people nonetheless.

We want to protect folks from alcoholism and drunkenness, so we tell them not to drink any alcoholic beverages. To protect them from alcohol, we recommend they avoid establishments that serve it. To be on the safe side, we tell them to avoid people who drink alcohol...and to avoid excessive laughter as you'd hear from tipsy people...and, in fact, to avoid parties in general except boring ones.

We want to protect folks from extramarital sex, so we create so much tension around the subject that we make people uncomfortable not only with the opposite sex, but with their own sexuality, too. Okay, we preachers admit, maybe we'll create a little sexual anxiety, maybe some of our hearers will become a tad nerdly, weird, uptight—but at least they won't get into overt sexual trouble. We hope.

We want to protect folks from following the crowd and succumbing to peer pressure, so we imply—or outright assert—that good Christians don't go to R-rated movies (or any movies at all), don't listen to rap music (or any popular music at all). We discourage them from making non-Christian friends. We approve them spending all their time in church services, church meetings, church activities—safe rabbit holes, a protective Christian ghetto.

We want to protect our folks from greediness—so we create a preaching climate that suggests it is morally and biblical dubious to make good money, to be extraordinarily successful, to maximize their earning potential. We imply that middle-class ambitions are okay, that mediocrity of any sort is safest.

We want to protect folks from losing their faith, so we warn them against reading philosophy, from participating in culture and the arts, from dealing with tough questions and controversial issues. We preachers exhort them to avoid the sciences (they might accept evolution!), avoid the social sciences (they might sympathize with liberals, criminals, and homosexuals!), avoid the arts (they may have to look at nudes!). We recite pat answers and platitudes, even when it makes us feel dishonest, shallow, trite, tortured. We feel justified, though, convincing ourselves that even a bad faith is better than a lost faith.

In short, wanting to protect our congregations from becoming of the world, we preachers tell them, "Don't be in it." We're just more comfortable to have Christians under our influence to be *outside* our culture rather than *in* it, *into* it, or *with* it.

There's only one problem: in trying to save people from the world, we miss the point. We actually ruin people (and ourselves) as disciples, and probably damage them as human beings, too. What's amazing is how patient our parishioners are with us, in light of the damage we do them. It's amazing how patient the Lord is with us too, in light of the damage we do to his people and his cause.

Preachers are certainly correct about Jesus calling us to be not *of* the world. We are correct about him wanting us to be different—like salt in the meat, not just meat; like light in the darkness, not just more darkness (Matthew 5:13ff).

But we're terribly wrong about the rest: Jesus did *not* want us to be *out* of the world—that's unquestionably clear from his prayer recorded in John 17. Like many preachers today, Jesus was concerned about our protection: "Father, protect them by the power of your name" (verse 11). But unlike many preachers today, he didn't try to guarantee that protection by isolating his followers. "My prayer is not that you take them out of the world," Jesus asked his Father, "but that you protect them from the evil one" (verses 14–16).

How then are we supposed to be in the world (not *planet*, but our *human culture*) without being conformed to it? There are two hints suggested in the next sentences of Jesus' prayer:

Hint one: "Sanctify them by the truth; your word is truth" (verse 17). *Sanctify* means *make holy* or *special*, or *set apart*. Jesus is saying that his followers are protected not by isolation, but by identity. Their very identity as disciples means they understand themselves to be set apart, called to a special and holy purpose. They have received the truth of God's message, and this truth has become for them a call to a higher, deeper, richer, more purposeful life.

So what does this look like today? Say I go to a movie. In this movie there are murderers, promiscuous sex addicts, thieves, and thugs. But among even these desperate and damaged characters, there are moments of tenderness, forgiveness, loyalty, honor, honesty. Watching all this, I look like everyone else in the theater, sitting there eating my popcorn and candy—but in my mind I am engaged in a kind of discernment that my movie-watching neighbors may be oblivious to. Because I have been set apart by God, I evaluate all I see and hear in the movie by the grid of his truth. The moviegoer next to me may be thinking, *Nice body...cool car...neat special effect.* But my mind is humming, comparing the action and values pictured in the movie with the message of truth I believe.

Hint two: "As you have sent me into the world," Jesus prayed, "I have sent them into the world" (verse 18).

To understand the immense significance of the word *sent* in Jesus' prayer, consider this scenario. In a seedy downtown club, there's a lot going on tonight: illicit drugs are being sold, bought, ingested...alcohol is being abused...prostitutes are soliciting and being solicited...gangs are planning violence.

Let's zoom in on four patrons in particular:

- Jake is looking for a hooker. He's lonely, desperate, and flush with cash after a robbery in another part of town.

- Shannelle is looking for a dealer. She's a heroin addict, and badly needs a hit. She was in treatment until yesterday, when she fled the treatment center. She's back on the street, broke, and asking herself what she's willing to do for a hit.

- Bruce is looking for an audience to show off for. He's got a lot of pent-up inferiority and aggression, and needs to impress somebody in order to feel good about himself. Maybe he can start a fight tonight.

- Donna is looking to hook up—friend or stranger, it really doesn't matter when you're this lonely, she thinks.

Over the next hour, stepping over empty bottles and litter, four other individuals enter the club. They look no different from the rest of the crowd milling around in the dim blue light of the club:

- Marcus is an undercover agent. He's looking for Jake, hoping to make an arrest.

- Charice is Shannelle's sister, and wants to convince her to go back into treatment.

- Leshawn is an AIDS activist. He's distributing pamphlets that urge people to avoid high-risk behaviors.

- Marie is a journalist, writing a story on the band playing on the stage.

The difference between the first and second group of patrons, of course, is that the second group are there on their own missions—and those missions make them *in* the club without being *of* it.

Similarly, with their minds transformed by such a sense of identity and mission, followers of Jesus can fully enter the world and live in it without becoming conformed to it. They don't enter the world alone, but they enter it and engage it with Jesus.

Consider Jesus:

- He was sent into the world as a seeker of lost treasures, a doctor to sick people, a friend to the friendless. Do we share his mission?

- He was an expression of God's love for the world. Could we be called the same?

- He wants to redeem and save the cultures of the world (as is made clear in passages like Revelation 5:9, where cultural distinctives are maintained in heaven). Do we similarly respect and love the world's diverse cultures?

- He attended parties and so was accused of being a drunk and a glutton, companion of tax collectors and other sinners. Are we too isolated to be similarly accused?

In one sense, we preachers are right: it's dangerous out there for Christians. It's easy to be conformed to the world, to lose our distinctive identity and mission.

But we preachers are missing the point when, instead of using all our powers and gifts to infuse people with a sense of Christian identity and mission, we opt for isolation. Whenever we offer the lesser option—and whenever people take it—we all fail Jesus, and our neighbors. We work against Jesus instead of for him.

I am reminded of a story Jesus told about violence and nudity as well as about compassion and kindness. Robbers beat up a traveler, stripped him, and left him dead on the shoulder of the road. Two highly religious people who came on the victim took the isolation option: they didn't feel comfortable coming near the beaten traveler, whose bloody and naked condition would be rated at least NC-17, and probably R. By the standards of many Christians today, that religious pair would be the good guys. Not in Jesus' version (which you can read in Luke 10:25ff).

There are two ways we can go wrong, the Scriptures point out. Living within our culture as we do, we can accommodate it, be infected with its evil, forget our unique identity, and thus become *of* it as well as *in* it. That's obviously tragic.

Or we can slide into the opposite and more subtle tragedy: we can isolate ourselves. Like the two religious men in Jesus' story, we can isolate in our holy huddle, our Christian ghetto (which, by denying our mission, becomes anti-Christian). Rather than being servants in our culture, doctors healing sickness, seekers after lost sheep, coins, and sons—we instead become an elitist clique, angry critics, snobs standing above culture, a frightened minority cringing outside it.

Jesus, on the other hand, inviting us to remember our identity and mission, wants us to join him in entering the world to enjoy and celebrate all that's good—and to seek to transform all that's not.

That means that whenever we hear a good song or see a good scene in a movie—whenever we enjoy good art or good cooking or find ourselves in good architecture or read a good paragraph in literature—whenever this happens, we celebrate that goodness, enjoy it, savor it, thank God for it. Christians aren't to be sourpusses and faultfinders, the apostle Paul wrote, because after all, "God has given us all things to enjoy" (1 Timothy 6:16-18) and "to the pure, all things are pure" (Titus 1:15). And we call a spade a spade when we see evil, corruption, dangerous philosophies, and destructive values—because God wants us to learn to "discern what is best" (Philippians 1:10), writes Paul.

If we live with this sense of identity and mission—if we remember who we are in the world and what we're about—we will be truly alive. If we don't—if we try to avoid sinful passions by extinguishing passion altogether, or try to isolate rather than enjoy and engage the world as followers and agents of Jesus—then we're missing the point. Jesus' followers are not to be isolated avoiders, passionless nerds, or snooty critics. They're to be in the world, into it—sent into it, in fact—with it, engaged, alive, passionate—not out of it. "Whoever claims to live in him," John the apostle wrote, "must walk as Jesus did" (1 John 2:6). Jesus was in the world, engaged, alive, involved, making a difference. So must we be.

How do we stay on track?

- *Live missionally.* Am I focused on Jesus' mission? Am I part of God's solution, or am I adding to human problems?

- *Live communally.* Am I hurting my Christian brothers and sisters, setting a bad example for them either by isolation or conformity? Am I listening to their warnings when I slip toward either danger? Am I helping my brothers and sisters guard themselves from both dangers?

- *Live spiritually.* Am I sensitive to the Holy Spirit, who constantly affirms my identity in Christ and constantly urges me to live missionally?

- *Live without judgment.* Can I believe the best about others without getting inquisitory with them—even if their way of living out their identity and mission in Christ is different than mine?

• *Live carefully*. Sin is tricky. Thousands of sexual addicts and drug addicts will tell you that what seems like freedom can become a new kind of bondage.

We walk a path that Jesus said is narrow. He wasn't legitimizing narrow-mindedness—quite the opposite, actually: Jesus told us that if we try to avoid the rattlesnake that is beside the path on the left, we'd better be careful not to edge too far over to the right either, because there's a crocodile in the bushes there. Narrow minds see only the dangers on one set of the narrow path; broad minds see both. That's our challenge if we don't want to miss the point.

Campolo Responds

Brian is quite right to call us away from any lifestyle that is disengaged from the culture in which we live. People miss the point if they confuse sanctification with culture-avoiding legalisms cultivated by our religious subculture.

But exactly *how* are we to be in the world? It has been said that it is one thing to go down into the cesspool (that is most modern entertainment) in order to cleanse it; it is another thing to go into the cesspool in order to take a bath. While Brian makes a good point for Christians going to movies, watching plays, and listening to rap music with great discernment in order to better understand our culture, I have to say that most of what comes across in the form of modern entertainment is trashy stuff and a waste of time. Not that I'm offended by a little bit of nudity, or shocked by scenes of violence; it's that most of what society offers up for our cultural digestion these days is just plain worthless. To act as though there is some profound truth waiting to be uncovered in cheap and tawdry stuff is hardly Christian.

Of course Christians should pay attention to good artistic expression because it can give insights into the values and mindsets that permeate our culture. If we are to speak to people who live in our society, we must be cognizant of what they are about. We cannot afford to ignore what is profoundly revealed in the arts. But let's be honest enough to say that most of the entertainment that comes across to us these days can hardly be called art.

If I had written this chapter, I would have explored the array of ways in which the evangelical community is being seduced by society into a cultural system that negates everything that Christianity is about—rather than being a leaven, transforming society into what it should be. Case in point: the consumerism that we so readily buy into, seeing as we do, no contradiction between our middle class materialistic values and what Jesus was all about. The fact that we so often are no different from the world in seeking spiritual and psychological gratification in the purchasing of consumer goods needs to be examined and properly exposed.

I'm sure that Brian would agree that, to a tragic degree, we have connected Christianity with American democratic capitalism, so that the two become indistinguishable ideologies. From what I observe, many evangelicals have lost the ability to distinguish between Americanism and Christian living. We have made Jesus into an American, so that when we go off to war (as we are very often prone to do these days), we are sure that God is on our side. "God created us in his image," George Bernard Shaw said, "and we decided to return the favor." That is more true than evangelicals are willing to admit.

In his discussion about conforming or isolating oneself from culture, I'm sure Brian would agree that Christians should stand over and against the society and call for changes that will deliver our educational system from the inefficiency that often leaves young people in poor communities without the educational tools to survive in our technologically sophisticated society. I wish he had attacked the racism and sexism that is inherent in our mores and folkways and had been more prophetic against a political-economic system in which the leaders of government and the leaders of big business and big unions have become so intertwined that government fails to serve the interests of the people in general.

In short, Christians should not affirm the culture as it is, but call it to become what Christ would have it be.

MISSING THE POINT:
Women in Ministry

Tony Campolo

- **Sharing speaking responsibilities** with me at a Bible conference a few years ago was a bright and articulate woman. Neither of us was prepared for the barrage of criticism that came from the conference's attendees, who felt that a female preacher at the conference was unbiblical.

- At a Seventh-day Adventist meeting I was surprised to learn that they did not ordain women—surprised, because their denomination was founded by a woman. The prophecies of Ellen White gave form to the SDA movement, and her teachings constitute the official creedal position of SDA churches.

- Many Baptist churches in 19th-century Maine and Wisconsin were pastored by women because no men were willing to take the positions. Yet many of those same churches today condemn the ordination of women, explaining away those older churches as mere splinter congregations.

- Growing up in an evangelical church, I regularly heard visiting missionaries speak to us. Many were women, who explained how they preached and planted churches in Africa, Latin America, and Asia. They were for the most part exciting preachers, whose zeal, gifts, and effectiveness were ample evidence that they had been called by God to do the work they were doing. Imagine my confusion when I learned that my church did not approve of the ordination of women.

I can imagine two reasons why evangelical churches would not ordain women who are equally as gifted as men who *are* ordained. Fear, for starters. If a man's masculinity depends on being dominant, then he will feel he's losing status in the eyes of other men if he is led by a woman. His self-worth is threatened when a woman is above him in a hierarchical system.

Often, of course, such reasons against ordaining women are masked by theological rationalizations generated by male chauvinists—and even by some women who find a variety of benefits for themselves in the traditional position that the church has prescribed for women.

The second reason I can imagine evangelical churches to oppose the ordination of women is a sincere belief that Scripture prohibits it. And I Timothy 2:11-12 is the most-quoted verse in defense of their prohibition:

> Let a woman learn in silence with full submission. I permit no woman to teach or to have authority over a man; she is to keep silent.

A casual reading of these verses does indeed seem to forbid women from even talking at church meetings, let alone be ordained as ministers. Yet the same church leaders who use this text to keep evangelical feminists out of formal church leadership are seldom inclined to fire all the female Sunday school teachers, youth directors, and Christian education directors from their staffs. They know only too well that church programs would fall apart without women.

So male church leaders are forced into some unconvincing double-talk: they distinguish between teaching and preaching. They allow women to teach. But preaching, which somehow implies an authority that teaching does not, is unbiblical for women to practice. How they can call this view biblical, I have not the faintest idea—for the apostle Paul recognizes no such distinction. A literal reading of these verses says simply that women should say nothing in church, period. No teaching, no preaching, no asking questions, no remarking.

Because I believe in the infallibility of the Scriptures, this passage posed a serious problem for me. Convinced as I am that the Holy Spirit guided Paul and kept him from errors, how could he have written something so unrealistic, so apparently misinformed and even mistaken?

Recent biblical scholarship, however, has demonstrated how little I understand what was going on in the first-century church. And I have lately come to read this passage with a whole new interpretation.

The upshot is that women in the early church were apparently abusing their newfound Christian freedom. The realization that in Christ there was neither male nor female (Galatians 3:28) and that before God women stood as equals with men—these new truths carried them into uncharitable and even shocking excesses. Even some evangelical scholars contend that these women, emancipated by their new status in Christ, were standing up in church meetings and lecturing their husbands about their behavior. Husband whose shortcomings were being publicly aired were humiliated, and the entire affair was becoming scandalous. Scholars believe that this was what Paul had in mind when he wrote,

> If there is anything they desire to know, let them ask their husbands at home.
> For it is shameful for a woman to speak in church.
> (1 Corinthians 14:35)

In this verse Paul was simply declaring that domestic problems should be dealt with in private, and that women should not with unseemly behavior abuse the liberties they had gained through Christ. If they had ideas about how their husband should and shouldn't treat them, church was not the place for them to try to teach their husbands what those husbands should and should not do.

Although I disagree with them, I admire the consistency of those Christians who sincerely believe the Bible forbids women from all leadership roles in the church. What bothers me— what, in fact, I think is utter hypocrisy—are those who readily allow women to be missionaries and preachers overseas, or encourage them to be Sunday school teachers here at home—yet contend that women should be silent in church services, should not teach men, and should not exercise any ecclesiastical authority over men.

New interpretations of Paul's letters aside, there are still other reasons for abandoning traditional prohibitions against the ordination of women.

I was surprised by what a couple of theologians told me—theologians from two of the nation's most theologically conservative seminaries. There was good reason to believe that Paul never intended that women be forever excluded from exercising leadership in church, they explained. It was clear to them from a careful study of the Scriptures that the apostle meant to prohibit women from preaching only in times and places where female leadership would scandalize the church in the eyes of society.

That is, if by exercising authority in the church, women created a barrier for non-Christians who would otherwise come to faith, then it was appropriate for women to refrain from such public leadership—usually preaching. But in today's world, these two theologians pointed out, keeping women out of pulpits is having the negative effect upon unbelievers' perception of the gospel—and therefore what worked in the first century can and ought to be set aside in this century.*

As much as this interpretation seems to be realistic and biblical, I still find it unacceptable, insofar as the tolerances of the current culture are said to determine the status of woman. As far as I am concerned, the rights of women established

*IRONICALLY, THESE TWO THEOLOGIANS WERE NOT WILLING TO GO PUBLIC WITH THE NAMES OF EITHER THEMSELVES OR THEIR SCHOOLS. IF THEY WERE IDENTIFIED WITH THIS PAULINE INTERPRETATION, THEY TOLD ME, THEIR SCHOOLS WOULD LOSE STUDENTS AND FINANCIAL SUPPORT. YET BOTH OF THESE PROFESSORS FELT THAT INTEGRITY WOULD NOT ALLOW THEM TO REMAIN SILENT MUCH LONGER. DURING THE NEXT FEW YEARS THEY WILL HAVE COMPLETED THE RESEARCH TO FULLY JUSTIFY THEIR CASE AND WILL THEN PUBLICLY CHALLENGE THEIR SEMINARIES AND STUDENTS TO RECONSIDER THEIR POSITIONS ON THE ORDINATION OF WOMEN.

through Christ are binding for all people, in all places, at all times.

The resurrection of Jesus dramatically demonstrates this changed status of women. At the moment of Jesus' death, the Bible tells us, there was an earthquake, and "the curtain of the temple was torn in two" (Luke 23:44). What curtain?

The temple on Mount Zion had three major sections. The innermost was the Holy of Holies, which contained the Ark of the Covenant, on which was located the mercy seat (Exodus 26:31-37). It was this chamber that the high priest would annually enter, on the Day of Atonement, and there pour the blood of a sacrificial lamb onto the mercy seat. This has been widely accepted as a symbol of the coming savior, the ultimate Lamb of God, whose shed blood would cover the sins of all people once and for all (Hebrews 10:10-12).

Outside of the Holy of Holies was the Holy Place, a section of the temple reserved for Jewish men—who in the Hebraic tradition were the first-class citizens of God's kingdom.

Take a step out of the Holy Place, and you were in the Outer Court, where Jewish women and Gentiles were assigned to worship. Literally, woman and Gentiles in ancient times were far off, in a place of inferiority, and denied the privileged status before the Lord that Jewish men possessed.

It was this curtain—which separated the Outer Court from the Holy Place—that was torn in two at the moment Jesus died. What divided Jewish men from Jewish women and Gentiles was ripped down. The system of stratification that Judaism had cultivated and that found expression in the temple was symbolically done away with.

The apostle Paul saw great significance in this event. To him the destruction of what separated Jewish men from others was evidence that the hierarchical system of the Old Testament had been abolished. The apostle writes,

> For [Christ] is our peace, in his flesh he has made both groups into one and has broken down the dividing wall, that is the hostility between us. He has abolished the law with its commandments and ordinances, that he might create in himself one new humanity in place of the two, thus making peace, and might reconcile both groups to God in one body through the cross, thus putting to death that hostility through it. (Ephesians 2:14-16)

For this reason, Paul writes to the Galatians,

> you are all children of God through faith, for all of you who were baptized into Christ have clothed yourselves with Christ. There is neither Jew nor Greek, neither slave nor free, neither male nor female, for you are all one in Christ Jesus. (3:26-28)

The subservience of women created by the sin of the first couple (Genesis 3:16) was abolished at the crucifixion, thanks to Christ, the second Adam, who voluntarily took on the work of the cross (Romans 5:12-21).

Elsewhere Paul acknowledged women as legitimate preachers when he advised them how to dress when they prophesy—which means to preach (1 Corinthians 11:5).

And in his letter to the Philippian Christians, Paul acknowledged the women Euodias and Syntyche as leaders and cofounders of that church (4:2-3).

Paul wasn't the only apostle to explain the new and equal spiritual status that Jesus gave women. In his Pentecost sermon, Peter points out that the work of the Holy Spirit was no longer limited by social, cultural, popular, or even traditional assumptions: for the gifts of the Spirit were imparted to females as well as to males.

> In the last days it will be, God declares, that I will pour out my Spirit upon all flesh, and your sons and your daughters shall prophesy, and your young men shall see visions, and your old men shall dream dreams. Even upon my slaves, both men and women, in those days I will pour out my Spirit; and they shall prophesy. (Acts 2:17-18)

People of all ages and both sexes would receive spiritual gifts that were to be used in Christian service—including prophesying, or preaching.

In his record of Acts, the writer Luke makes it clear that the husband-wife team of Aquila and Priscilla taught Apollos his theology, even correcting him in what he was preaching (Acts 18:26). The four daughters of Philip, furthermore, became preachers (Acts 21:9).

In the face of such blatant scriptural evidence for the ordination of women, opponents are known to bend Scripture to suit their own adamant opinions. In Romans 16:7, for instance, Paul sends greetings to *Junias* whom he recognizes as an apostle. But that's not a good translation of the name. Uncomfortable with the implications of a female holding the highest preaching office in the church, the mostly male translators of many Bible versions render the name as the masculine *Junias*. Fortunately there are better translations—like the new TNIV—that recognize the apostle as *Junia*, a female (sometimes translated *Julia*). When men start imposing translations on the Bible that agree with their theology, they are walking on thin ice.

I thank God for the straightforward New Testament message that women and men in Christ are spiritual equals. For the biblical message only seconds the incredible leadership that women have given the church throughout history:

- Kathryn Kuhlman, the American preacher and healer

- The wonderful uniformed women of the Salvation Army, who so faithfully have declared the message of salvation as they cheerfully lived out Christian charity toward the poor

- Antoinette L. Brown, America's first fully ordained woman

135

- Phoebe Palmer, the feminist who wrote *Promise of the Father*

- Christabel Pankhurst, Christian leader of the British suffrage movement, who faithfully preached God's Word

...and countless others, in all parts of the world.

A Roman Catholic bishop once explained to me how women had been a godsend to rural churches in his diocese that lacked priestly leadership. Nuns visited the sick, taught the catechism, preached the homilies, and even served Holy Communion. In short, these sisters served as pastors, although the people did not call them pastors. When I suggested that since these nuns did everything that priests do and therefore deserved to be ordained, he agreed.

"And most people in these parishes agree, too," he said. "But you know how the church is."

Unfortunately, I do. Yet women are gradually becoming more and more evident in American church leadership. In some ways we are just beginning to recognize what it meant when Christ changed the status of women. There is every cultural and scriptural reason for women—who are spiritual equals with men—to minister according to their giftedness, even when those gifts are public preaching gifts.

McLaren Responds

I was discipled in very conservative evangelical settings, where our Bible teachers prided themselves on *not* being liberal, on sticking to a literal interpretation of the Bible. And *literal* meant (for most of them) that one didn't ask questions about context or culture or intent or purpose: one just read the words as if they were written in a legal document, and followed the "letter of the law." *Liberal* meant any other kind of reading.

So "liberal" and "literal" were your only two choices when it came to interpreting the Bible, and the "literal" interpretation was the restrictive one for women in evangelical churches. Something inside me felt that this approach was legally safe but morally dangerous. There had to be a third alternative to liberal or literal.

I found it when I read 1 Corinthians 9, where Paul explains his missionary strategy. "To the Jews I became like a Jew," he says. To the Greeks, he became like a Greek. He had the flexibility to engage with anyone, in any culture, for the sake of the gospel. If Paul were living in my world, I thought, working and ministering in a highly educated, post-industrial society where men and women are treated (or are supposed to be treated) as equals in every area of life—where failing to treat men and women as equals would be as offensive as practicing racism or forcing eight-year-old children to work in coal mines— wouldn't Paul apply that same missionary strategy? Wouldn't the same strategy require him to *affirm* women in leadership rather than restrict them? After all, he had said "in Christ there is no...male or female."

137

restriction on women simply an inescapable accommodation to the prevailing culture?

In other words, to be faithful to Paul's underlying strategy of cultural penetration and engagement across cultures, wouldn't one be forced, under different cultural circumstances, to do the very opposite of what Paul did in his own cultural circumstances?

When I asked myself this question, and answered it, I was given permission to step onto new ground when it came to women in ministry. And having taken that step, it felt to me, to go back would be like stepping back into slavery, or back into child labor, or back into racism.

I have two gifted daughters, young women with wonderful potential to serve God and the church. Whether God has called them into what is known as "professional Christian ministry," I don't know. But I am quite certain that if so called, they would be great pastors or elders or whatever, as gifted and qualified as any man. At the church I serve, we have been blessed for many years to have women working as equal partners with men throughout church life—and I know that in this environment my daughters will have every opportunity to use all their gifts to the full. I hope that readers of this chapter of Tony's will be influenced to create similar environments.

I am meeting more and more female pastors and church planters these days. They are pioneers, courageous trailblazers, as are the men in privileged positions who encourage them, make way for them, defend them from sniping by others who don't understand. I hope this chapter will encourage readers to realize that the priesthood of all believers is not the priesthood of all *male* believers, but will instead find a better way of treating our sisters—a way that unleashes them for ministry that benefits the whole church and world, a way of reading the Bible that is superior to either "liberal" or "literal."

MISSING THE POINT:
Leadership

Brian D. McLaren

I admit it: I spent most of the '80s and early '90s wishing I could fulfill the CEO model of Christian leadership. CEOs made it. They were unflinchingly confident, powerful, knowledgeable, larger than life. I admired such CEO-model leaders in Christendom, I attended their seminars, and returned home wildly inspired and mildly depressed. If you've been to such seminars, you know the feeling.

I mean, think of David trying on King Saul's armor. Imagine David, at that time probably a size M or even an S guy, going into battle with Goliath with Saul's XXL armor. He would have been opened and eaten up like a can of sardines.

I wasn't the only one who thought that the best image of the successful pastor was the CEO, the alpha male, the armored knight, the corporate hero. Thousands of us tried on that armor, and the results—in our churches and in our personal lives—weren't pretty. Of course, the suit fit a few of us—many leaders really *are* XXLs—but most of us eventually realized that if we were going to be of any use to God, we'd better be ourselves. (A novel idea!)

About the time I was reaching that conclusion, I was rethinking a lot of things. I was seeing modernity give way to a new matrix or pattern, and was surprised to see snugly my whole understanding of Christianity fit within the modern matrix. I wondered how ministry, theology, spirituality, and evangelism would change as the matrix changed.

And I wondered, too, how leadership would change.

Somewhere in the middle of these musings, I remembered the scene in *The Wizard of Oz* when Toto pulls back the curtain to reveal that the great Wizard of Oz is a rather normal guy hiding behind an imposing image. It struck me that the world of the 1940s reflected in that film was in many ways a world at the height of modernity, a world enamored with Superman, the Lone Ranger, with Great Men. And it struck me that by exposing the

Wizard as a fraud, the film was probing an unexpressed cultural doubt, giving voice to a rising misgiving, displaying an early pang of discontent with its dominant model of larger-than-life leadership.

And it made me wonder what image of leadership would replace the great Wizard.

The answer, of course, appeared in the next scene. The leader wasn't the lion, the scarecrow, or the tin man. It was Dorothy.

At first glance, Dorothy is all wrong as a model of leadership. She is the wrong gender (female) and the wrong age (young). Rather than being a person with all the answers, who is constantly informed of what's up and what's what and where to go, she is herself lost, a seeker, vulnerable, often bewildered. These characteristics would disqualify her from modern leadership. But they serve as her best credentials for leadership in the emerging culture.

In the world of Christian ministry, we can identify 10 wizardly characteristics of high modern leadership. (My use of the masculine pronoun in this list is deliberate.)

Bible analyst. The modern Christian leader dissects the Bible like a scientist dissects a fetal pig: to gain knowledge through analysis. And in modernity, knowledge is power.

Broadcaster. In modernity, when one amplifies his voice electronically and adds a little reverb, his power quotient goes way up. Being slick, being smooth, being big, being on the air—that's what makes you a leader.

Objective technician. The organization (church, ministry, et cetera) is a machine, and the leader knows how to work the machine, how to make it run, how to tweak it, how to engineer or reengineer it. He's the subject, and the organization is the object.

Warrior-salesman. Modern leadership is about conquest—
"winning souls," launching "crusades," "taking" this city
(campus, whatever) for Jesus, et cetera. It's about
marketing, getting buy-in, and selling. (And sometimes
selling out.)

Careerist. The modern leader grasps the bottom rung of
the ladder, and—earning his credentials along the way—
climbs, climbs, and climbs. This is as true for young
preacher boys on the rise as it is for young stockboys who
would be CEOs.

Problem solver. Bring it to him, and he'll fix it. Come to
him, and he'll fix you.

Apologist. He'll tell you why he's right, and why your
doubt or skepticism is wrong.

Threat. A powerful and underrated weapon of the modern
Christian leader: the threat of exclusion. Through mocking
caricatures or other rhetorical forms of demonization, a
gifted orator (or editor) can make you fear that if you don't
agree with (or follow or submit to) his leadership, you'll be
slashed from the membership list and banished—like the
Wizard bellowing threats from behind his curtain.

Knower. The modern Christian leader is supremely
confident in his opinions, perspectives, beliefs, systems,
and formulations. While the rest of us question and doubt,
he is the answer-man who really *knows*.

Solo act. There's only room for one in the Wizard's
control booth—and there's only room for one at the top of
the church organizational chart.

Dorothy as a leadership model, on the other hand, is very different. Instead of manipulating images in a control booth,

she's stuck in a predicament—still a little dizzy from the torna-
do, lost, and far from home. As she sets out on her journey,
she finds other needy creatures—one lacking courage, another
lacking intelligence, another lacking a heart. Some help! Yet
she believes that their needs can be fulfilled on a common
quest, and her earnestness, her compassion, her determination, and her youthful spunk galvanize them into a foursome
(five, with Toto), singing down the Yellow Brick Road together.

Dorothy doesn't have the knowledge to help them avoid all
problems and dangers...she doesn't protect them from all threats
and temptations. But neither does she give up. Her passion
remains strong, and in the end they all get what they need.

Maybe one of the film's many enduring delights is hidden in
Dorothy's unwizardly leadership charisma. Maybe people in the
1940s were just beginning to yearn for a way of leadership that
now is becoming attractive to many of us: a post-wizard kind of
leadership.

> **Bible analyst > Spiritual sage.** As we move beyond
> modernity, we lose our infatuation with analysis,
> knowledge, information, facts, belief systems—and with
> those who traffic in them. Instead we are attracted to
> leaders who possess that elusive quality of wisdom (think
> James 3:13-18), who practice spiritual disciplines, whose
> lives are characterized by depth of spiritual practice (not
> just by the tightness of belief system). These leaders possess
> a moral authority more closely linked to character than to
> intellectual credentials...they are more sages than
> technicians...it's their slow, thoughtful, considered answer
> that convinces, not the answer-man-know-it-all-ness.
> Dorothy has a softer authority—a reflection of her
> earnestness and kindness—not an intellectual domination.

Broadcaster > Listener. In the emerging culture it's not how loud you shout that counts—it's how deeply you listen. Just as Dorothy engages her traveling companions by listening to their stories and evoking their needs, leaders of the emerging culture create a safe place that attracts a team, and then those leaders empower their teams by the amazing power of a listening heart.

Objective technician > Spiritual friend. Think of the difference between a scientist objectively studying chimpanzees and a crusader dedicated to saving them from extinction. One is cool-headed, detached, analytical; the other, warm-hearted, involved, passionate. In modernity a leader coolly leads his organization, detached from it the way an machine operator is detached from his machine, viewing it as one more stop in his journey to complete a career. But on this side of the transition, leaders love their teams, and those to whom their teams are sent, with a crusader's passion and a lover's attachment. (Or, more perversely put—in high modernity, I Corinthians 13 would read, "If I have all love and would lay down my life for my friends, but have not analytical managerial knowledge and detached leadership technique, I am a poor excuse for a leader." Beyond modernity, we return toward Paul's original meaning.)

Warrior-salesman > Dancer. In a world plagued by ethnic hatred and telemarketers, every strident voice that adds sales pressure to the world is one voice too many. People don't want to be "won to Christ" or "taken for Jesus" in a "crusade." Neither do they want to be subjected to a sales pitch for heaven, that sounds for all the world like an invitation to check out a time-share resort. (*It's absolutely free!*) A presentation of the gospel that sounds like a

145

military ultimatum or like a slick sales pitch will dishonor the gospel for people in the emerging culture. Instead, think of leadership—and especially evangelism—as a dance. A leader hears the music that I don't hear, and she knows how to move to its rhythm. Gently, she helps me begin to hear its music, feel its rhythm, and learn to move to it with grace and joy.

Careerist > Amateur. The root of the word *amateur* is *amare*, to *love*. Most of us in Christian leadership know that ministry as a career can quickly quench the motivation of love. The professionalization of ministry will be one of the dark legacies of modernity, I believe—a classic case of jumping from the frying pan of medieval clericalism into the fire of professionalism. How can we keep our higher motivation alive? How can Christian leadership be less like the drudgery of a job and more like the joy of a day golfing or hiking or fishing or playing soccer or whatever...not something we *have* to do, but something we *get* to do?

Problem solver > Quest inspirer. The man-at-the-top of modern leadership is the guy you go to for answers and solutions. There are times, no doubt, when that's what we need now, too. But postmodern leaders will be as interested in creating new problems, in setting new challenges, in launching new adventures as in solving, finishing, or facilitating old ones. Dorothy does exactly this: she helps her companions trade their old problems (birds landing on the scarecrow, the tin man being paralyzed by rust, the lion faking bravado) for a new quest. This, of course, is what Jesus does, too: not solve the problems of the Pharisees (*How can we get these stupid crowds to know and obey the law as we do?*), but create new problems (*Seek first the kingdom of God...*).

Apologist > Apologizer. Instead of defending old answers, the new kind of leader will often apologize for how inadequate they are. In modernity, you gained credibility by always being right; in the emerging culture, you gain authority by admitting when you're wrong and apologizing humbly. Think of the Pope's visit to the Middle East in early 2000. Sincere apology is essential to the new apologetic; we Christians will need to repent before we can ask anyone else to do so. Such humility and vulnerability was one of Dorothy's most winsome and leaderly characteristics.

Threat > Includer. If Dorothy poses any threat, it is the threat of inclusion, not of exclusion. She threatens you with acceptance—you're part of her journey, a member of her team. Unless, of course, you refuse and walk away. That kind of leadership strikes me as gospel leadership, and it reminds me of Someone Else.

Knower > Seeker. Dorothy's appeal as a leader arises, ironically, from her being lost and being passionate about seeking a way home. Did it ever strike you odd that in contemporary Christian jargon, it's the pre-Christians who are called seekers? Where does that leave the Christians? Shouldn't Christian leaders be the lead seekers?

Solo act > Team builder. All along her journey, Dorothy welcomed company. She was glad for a team. By the end of their journey, the lion, the scarecrow, and the tin man have joined Dorothy as peers, partners, friends. Her style of leadership was empowering, ennobling—not patronizing or paternalistic. Her style didn't create dependency. So effective was her empowering of them that, after a tearful goodbye, they moved on to their own adventures.

So why take a silly kid's movie so seriously, you ask. You're right—it's just a movie. But I find the film's repudiation of traditional, modern leadership to be fascinating, and maybe an early expression of a cultural shift that we are more fully experiencing today than when the film was produced.

Ultimately, of course, I find in Dorothy's way of leadership many echoes of our Lord's. After all, *can you* imagine the great and terrible Oz washing his subjects' feet? Or his voice booming out from behind the curtain, "I no longer call you servants, but friends"?

Maybe some of us are trying hard to be something we're not. Maybe we're imitating styles of leadership that are inappropriate to our identity or setting—that are even inappropriate to the gospel. Maybe the best thing that could happen to us would be to have the curtain pulled back to reveal us not as XXL superheroes, but regular size M men and women. Maybe then, with the amplifiers turned off and the imaged dropped, we can admit we've been missing the point about leadership, and we'll hear Jesus inviting us to learn new ways of leading in his cause.

Campolo Responds

I sense that Brian wants church leaders to broaden their options beyond the CEO leadership model and strive simply to be ourselves as we lead. Christian leadership is all about discovering our personal traits and gifts and using them as best we can to help others.

Granted, it would be well if every one of us took time off to evaluate who and what we are so that we might live out such a challenge—especially in the light of 1 Corinthians 11, where St. Paul admonishes us to not neglect the gifts we have.

Brian recommends Dorothy of *The Wizard of Oz* as an alternative model of leadership for our postmodern culture, but we also need to be careful that we don't overreact against the CEO model and slip into what William White, Jr., called "the organization man" style of leadership, which can contribute to camaraderie and a sense of well-being among employees but lacks entrepreneurial genius and genuine creativity. Dorothy is a lot of fun and makes her partners on the yellow brick road feel good, but she is not what you would want in a leader, say, during a time of crisis.

German sociologist Max Weber makes it clear that different kinds of leaders are needed in different kinds of situations. When an organization (like a church) is in crisis, Weber contends—when there is disorganization and confusion, when patterns and norms are jumbled—what is needed is a charismatic personality, a leader who can propose a new vision for the future and convince other people that such a vision can be realized. Leaders like these, Weber writes, seem to be imbued with an authority that comes from beyond themselves (think of

Joan of Arc or, in an ultimate sense, Jesus). Such leaders are not so much creators of organizations as they are creators of movements. Charismatic leaders generate enthusiasm and inspire total commitment. (But they do not necessarily have to be good people. Hitler was an incredible leader who generated among the dispirited German people a genuine sense of purpose. Yet he was evil to the core.)

If we are to believe the Bible, it is charismatic leaders that God raises up in times of crisis. In the book of Judges, we read of several strong, decisive leaders that God appointed to lead Israel to glorious deliverance from the predicaments in which they found themselves (Samson, Gideon, Deborah, et cetera). These charismatic leaders were not team builders or great listeners, as Barnabas seems to have been—but there are moments in the life of the church when a charismatic leader is needed more than a consensus builder.

All of us have seen organizations that had the wrong kind of leader, given the organization's situation at the moment. In short, having the ideal leader usually means having the right person at the right time. It is no coincidence that Jesus was born, says Scripture, "in the fullness of time"—biblical language for what Weber called *elective affinity*, that is, some kind of functional fit between a leader and the social situation into which that leader is placed. How many people go into the pastorate and end up in churches where they ought not to be *at that time*—churches where other kinds of leaders would have done brilliantly?

The charismatic leader that Weber describes is only one of what he calls the "ideal types" of leaders; there are others. At other times a "Dorothy" is needed, as Brian writes. And although church leaders are better leaders when they are themselves, they should recognize that there are many different kinds of leaders. It is important for church leaders to ask themselves, *Am I what this church needs at this particular place, and at this particular time? Or does this church need a different kind of leader?*

MISSING THE POINT:
Seminary

Tony Campolo

I remember when I told D. W. Huggard, the African-American pastor of Philadelphia's Mt. Carmel Baptist Church, that I was going to seminary.

"Be careful," he warned. "Seminary can take the steam out of a preacher. When they finish with you, you might not have the power to preach the fuzz off of a peach."

Seminary can do that to you. It can intellectualize religious experience, in the process diminishing one's zeal. For too many, in fact, the seminary experience fosters more doubt than faith. Worst of all, seminary can nurture students in an attitude of spiritual superiority.

Don't get me wrong—seminary per se is not a waste of time. It has several advantages, and can do you more than a little good.

Seminary can put you in touch with great scholars. It was in seminary that I met and studied under Norman H. Maring, professor of church history, who taught me the value of scholarship. He taught me by example how to think critically, how to interpret Scripture within the context of church tradition, how to culturally conceptualize the message of the gospel.

Nothing matches the privilege of sitting under the tutelage of a professor like Maring. It doesn't matter what the course is—learning at the feet of a great scholar marks a student forever. If you find yourself in seminary, concern yourself not so much with what courses you take, but from whom you take them. You'll forget most subject matter within a decade, but the influence of a memorable instructor stays with you for life.

Seminary can provide you with a network of lifelong ministerial friends. At seminary you will come to know those men and women who most likely will be your colleagues in ministry for the rest of your life. The trust that grows between seminary classmates can create a lifelong network of support that is invaluable in times of trouble (and trouble is inevitable, in ministry as in all of life). Plus, if you belong to a denomination that requires your attendance at denominational conferences, the prospect of reconnecting with old friends is all that makes the meetings tolerable.

The ministry tends to be a lonely profession. Seminary can help here, offering a camaraderie that can continue beyond one's classroom years into many decades of close friendships. Fortunate are the ministers who have longstanding ministerial friends to whom they can turn when the perplexities of the ministry are overwhelming.

Seminaries are the first stop for search committees looking for new ministers. This is true whether a search committee is looking for a new graduate, or for referrals to experienced alumni already out serving churches. Placement offices of seminaries usually have enough information about their graduates to suggest a good fit for a seeking church. Seminaries have long memories—which means that seminary-trained ministers have an advantage in landing jobs.

Especially if you have your sights set on a job in your denominational hierarchy, you need a seminary degree. Which, incidentally, is not an exercise in futility, for all the dark talk one may hear about denominational bureaucracies. Those in denominational leadership can often give new and decisive direction to the church as it seeks to impact the world of the 21st century. Take Bob Edgar, CEO of the National Council of Churches (and a seminary grad), who is successfully forging the NCC into a major force in alleviating poverty both in the U.S. and the third world. As an executive in an ecclesiastical bureaucracy, Edgar is making a huge difference for the kingdom of God.

These benefits notwithstanding, a seminary education won't make you into a preacher. *Preaching comes as a gift, not with a degree*. Paul's words in Ephesians 4:11 imply as much. Yes, scholarship can provide content for sermons. Yes, courses in homiletics can sharpen your abilities and polish your delivery. But in the end, if you haven't got the gift of preaching, you will not be effective in the pulpit.

Yet evangelical seminaries in particular only feed this problem when they make enrollment an individual, autonomous decision. If you show up in your pastor's study and announce that you feel called by God to go into the ministry, it is not likely that you will be discouraged, or even questioned beyond some cursory examination of your motives. When your decision is announced to the church, any doubts parishioners may have about your suitability for the ministry will probably go unspoken. "Who am I to question another's calling from God?" they think.

They are *exactly* the ones to either question or affirm the call of another to ministry. In the early church it was the congregation that decided who would and would not be chosen for the ministry of preaching. It was the church that set aside Paul and Barnabas for the ministry, not merely the desire of those two to preach the gospel. For it takes the accountability of a group to deal with not only the theology of a call, but with the psychology. Is the claimant mistaking ego needs for a call from God? Is the call primarily a subconscious sense of obligation generated by a parent? Or is the claimant attempting to compensate for feelings of guilt? A congregation, rather than the prospective seminarians themselves, is usually better able to determine the validity of a call to preach.

There are theological grounds, too, for the church doing the choosing. When two or three are gathered together in Jesus' name, he said, he is especially present among them (Matthew 18:20). There is much guidance and decision-making help implied in this concept. Generally speaking—and particularly in the case of a perceived call to preach—the will of God can best be discerned when the corporate body of Christians pray themselves to a sense of unanimity.

The calling of George W. Truett illustrates the advantages of a preaching call confirmed by a body of Christians instead of simply and autonomously decided by one who desires the job. Truett was a Texas lawyer and a member of the First Baptist Church of Dallas when that congregation went looking for a new pastor. Church members considered several candidates—then settled on Truett of all people, despite the fact that he was neither seminary trained nor ordained. He declined, said he did not want the job. But the congregation persisted: they had prayed about this, they said, and frankly were convinced it was God's will that Truett be their pastor. All they wanted to know was how he could refuse the call, seeing what God had revealed to the church. Truett eventually capitulated, accepted the call, and led the church as it became one of the greatest in America.

It's the gift that makes the preacher—and in this case the congregation knew better than the individual so gifted.

This is not to say that, blessed with the gift of preaching, you need not bother with study and training. Study to show yourself approved unto God, Paul wrote to his protégé Timothy (2 Timothy 2:15). Still, in my observation what seminaries *do* have you study is not always what best equips you for the preaching ministry.

Language classes in Hebrew and Greek are still required in most seminaries, with the assumption that preachers need to read and study the Bible in its original languages. The reality? Very, very few preachers read and study the Bible in Hebrew and Greek after they graduate. They do a fine job interpreting the Bible for their congregations with commentaries in their own languages (written by experts in ancient languages) interpreting scripture for their congregations.

What if the credits eaten up by subjects seminarians seldom if ever use after graduation were instead devoted to more subjects they will actually need in churches—like business and marketing courses? It is not true that with a gifted preacher, a church will inevitably grow. Good sermons may get visitors to stay once they come, but getting folks to come in the first place may take some marketing expertise.

It was a marketing degree, not an M.Div., that Bill Hybels had when he launched the tiny fellowship that would one day be Willow Creek Community Church. It's not that Hybels is a theological lightweight, contrary to some critics. His sermons are biblically sound and brilliantly relevant to the needs of his congregation—and the relevance comes not from giftedness or theological discernment, but from thoughtfully studying his congregation. As any good marketer would, Hybels deliberately surveys his people with questionnaires in order to determine what they worry about, what their needs are, what's most important to them. During the summer months he reflects on their responses, studies the Bible for how it speaks to their issues, and reads extensively about these same issues. Then he schedules what subjects he will preach on in the coming year, and circulates the schedule to those on his team responsible for music and drama in the services.

The result is preaching that is utterly biblical and acutely relevant. But the process isn't something you'll learn in most seminaries. Maybe it's time that some business school courses find their way into seminary.

And not just marketing, but how about a course or two in conflict resolution? Seminaries are inclined to give their students the impression that if they pray enough and seek a close spiritual relationship with God, they can avoid most conflicts in their churches. Big misconception. Congregations are filled with well-meaning people with different ideas about what is best for the church, and one faction or another is usually making some sort of power play. What preachers need is not unlike what business students study: how to resolve conflicts between labor and management. Such courses would go a long ways toward helping ministers defuse volatile situations in their churches.

Not only do seminaries tend to require the wrong subjects. They seldom structure their academic programs and course requirements according to a rapidly changing world.

At a conference of United Methodist Church ministers, a bishop punched the air with his fist as he proclaimed, "If the 1950s ever come back again, WE'RE READY!" The good news was that he was speaking facetiously; the bad news was that the statement was true. Seminaries as well as denominations suffer from this kind of cultural lag. What occasional changes they do make to their curriculums are never enough, and never frequent enough to keep their students abreast of the world into which those students will soon graduate and begin working.

Geno-ethics

For some time we have been genetically modifying our foods. Of late we have finally broken the human genetic code, making it possible to determine what kinds of people will inhabit our planet in future generations. IQs can be predetermined. Soon, we are told, we will be able to eliminate genetic propensities for most diseases, extend life expectancy to beyond a hundred years, diminish tendencies to certain antisocial behaviors, and even genetically program one's attitude toward religion.

Or take the highly controversial subject of homosexual orientation: there is growing speculation that homosexual tendencies are programmed in the fetus by one gene. Such an idea has huge implications in both mainline and evangelical churches. Should we turn this gene off, so to speak—an ability we are quickly developing—or should we affirm homosexuality by not interfering with what is apparently designed by nature?

Genetics intersects with ethics in other areas, too. How should a pastor go about premarital counseling if, through genetic testing, it is determined the would-be husband will probably die of a heart attack before he reaches 45? Or if it is likely that any children born to this marriage will have major or minor birth defects?

Computers and A.I.

Seminaries are not yet training their students to live and pastor in a society where computers replicate humans in more and more aspects—even someday assuming emotions like love, joy, and spiritual ecstasy. In *The Age of Spiritual Machines*, Ray Kurzweil raises questions about the uses of computers—not technical questions, but some heavy theological issues that not even divinity schools are exploring yet.

Rudimentary technology is already in place, Kurzweil points out, whereby brain waves can be traced and then downloaded onto a computer disk. Which raises the question: if the function of all your organs can be artificially simulated, and your thoughts and emotions downloaded to a computer—will this new you be you? Where is the soul in all this?

Geopolitics and Religio-Cultural Issues

How many seminaries lead their students in processing the ideas of Samuel P. Huntington, a Harvard University political science professor who contends that the whole geopolitical landscape has changed from an ideological struggle between communism and capitalism to a struggle between cultures in general, and between religions specifically? The violent confrontations of the last decade have been largely between fundamentalist groups of opposing religious beliefs; what seminaries provoke their students to explore such things?

Karl Barth said that a preacher should be able to develop a sermon with a Bible in one hand and the day's newspaper in the other. Frankly, I do not think that seminaries pay enough attention to the newspaper.

And if seminaries continue to distance themselves from the real and relevant world into which their students will graduate? Consider an alternative: home-trained preachers.

Some of the most influential theological education in the early 18th century took place without seminaries, without formal training, without degrees. Take William Tennant, who served a church in Bucks County, Pennsylvania. Tennant built a log cabin behind his home and there gave personal instruction and practical experience to a handful of young men. These "home schooled" preachers, imbued with evangelical passion, were the triggers of the Great Awakening—perhaps the greatest spiritual revival America has ever known.

They had their enemies. The traditionally educated clergy of the Presbyterian Synod of New Jersey did everything they could to keep those new preachers out of churches lest, as they feared, "the ministry be deluged with half-educated enthusiasts." But Tennant's "Log College" alumni had already gained such widespread support that there was no stopping them.

This model is viable for ministerial training today, and in some cases is already in place. I could name a half dozen pastors who have made their churches into ministry training centers, especially for pastoral candidates within their own congregations. With distance-learning programs and the Internet, such candidates need not set foot on a seminary campus, yet they can acquire all the subject matter they'd receive in a traditional seminary experience. Add practical experience and mentoring by a seasoned pastor, and home training of this sort could be the best option for the education of many ministers.

The gift, not a seminary degree, makes the preacher. Yet seminary is often a wise means (though hardly the only means) for perfecting one's calling to preach the truth of God's kingdom.

I never received formal seminary training. Like many church planters, I got into pastoral work accidentally by starting an evangelistic Bible study in my home, which evolved into a house church, which eventually invited me to be its pastor. Although my leadership training came on the job and not through traditional or certified channels, it has nevertheless been rigorous and energetic, demanding, and ongoing. I've learned many lessons the hard way.

Do I wish I had attended seminary? Not for one minute.

Don't get me wrong: I am pro-education. Before entering pastoral ministry full-time, I was a college English teacher. I believe in education. My primary complaint about the current seminary system, however, is that it too often is a system of certification, not education. Not always, but too often seminaries recruit students who already know what they think and are not interested in having their thinking stretched or challenged, thank you very much. They'd rather learn stronger defenses and justifications and proofs for their current beliefs. Denominations, churches, and donors, meanwhile, commonly expect affiliated seminaries to confirm students in the stretch-resistant beliefs they came with, and seminary boards seek to satisfy those expectations.

Meanwhile, as Tony says, the church faces intense new questions, profound new challenges—but our seminaries too often continue certifying people who are insufficiently educated to face those new challenges. We teach them what to think, not how to think; or we obsessively teach them how to answer yesterday's questions while failing to face today's and or to anticipate tomorrow's. I read recently that GRE scores for incoming seminarians have been slipping for many years, now averaging below the "combined 1000" mark—which suggests that our brightest young Christians do not consider seminary (or, by implication, church ministry) an attractive place of worthwhile challenge. I know that is how I felt when I considered attending seminary in my twenties.

But the proper response to this crisis is not more or less formal education, but *better* and *different* kinds of education. In other words, education isn't the problem: the problem is the standard forms of formal education.

Which brings me to my second complaint about our current seminary system. Better and different kinds of leadership training for the church's leaders will integrate theology and spirituality, ecclesiology and missiology, scholarship and community. For without a balanced passion for spirituality, mission, and community (as well as for theology, ecclesiology, and scholarship), we certify scholars, debaters, and talking heads—not multidimensional leaders in the way of Jesus Christ.

What will these different and better kinds of spiritual formation and leadership training look like? Here's my guess:

- Tomorrow's new breed of seminarians will remain more integrated with the life of the local church, so their training will be on the job, connected with real-life situations and street-level people. If they can't get along with and prove themselves truly helpful to a community of ordinary folks, their academic achievements will earn the negligible credit they deserve.

- The training of tomorrow's seminarians will be more akin to the apprenticeship model, where professors become mentors, who train by their lives and their daily, ongoing example, instead of by just their lecture notes.

- The learning of tomorrow's seminarians will take the shape of a life-long course in dynamic learning communities (think of the latent implications and images in the word *course*), rather than of front-loaded information dumps in theory-laden classes of disconnected students (think of the latent implications and images in the word *classes*).

- The training of tomorrow's seminarians will be more attuned to the flow of history, more conscious of the unfolding story of Christianity across cultures over time, instead of being cramped in the boxy abstractions of modern analysis or the rigid mechanisms of modern systematics.

- Tomorrow's seminarians will be more sensitive to contemporary culture and contemporary issues.

- The training of tomorrow's seminarians will be more global and missional, requiring them to experience life and mission among the urban or rural poor in at least one cross-cultural setting.

- Tomorrow's seminarians will prove themselves proficient in the habitual practice of spiritual disciplines in a community of practitioners, so that an authentic spirituality infuses all they do.

- Tomorrow's seminarians will include women who are welcomed as partners in ministry, not as second-class citizens. Furthermore, Christian learning communities will strive to reflect

the diversity and equality of the kingdom of God by welcoming
minorities and leaders from other cultures.

I'm glad to say that I see several intrepid seminaries responding to
current deficiencies and exploring new possibilities in innovative ways.
We have a long way to go, but important first steps are being taken.
Maybe a next step will be for more of us pastors to follow the example
of William Tennant and build some "log colleges" in our back yards—
each with a T-1 line that links them to a consortium of innovative
seminaries.

MISSING THE POINT:
Environmentalism

Tony Campolo

Christians have let New Agers hijack the environmentalist movement and make it their own domain. Environmentalism
should be a Christian concern.

All creation is waiting for the sons and daughters of God to
rescue it from the painful suffering it has had to endure at the
hands of those of us who have been neglectful and destructive,
wrote the apostle Paul in Romans 8. And being filled with the
Holy Spirit, he wrote in that same chapter of the Bible,
involves joining with God in rescuing nature from an
exploitative urban industrial society.

The two biggest reasons why Christians should make
environmentalism a high priority, however, are that Christian
stewardship requires it, and that the destruction of the earth's
natural beauty actually impacts the worship of God.

Christians Should Make Environmentalism a High Priority Because Christian Stewardship Requires It

In the Genesis story we are ordered by God to care for creation
(1:28-31). In the Torah's jubilee passage (Leviticus 25:3-7),
Israel was required to ensure that the land was not exhausted
through overuse, and that the land have a fallow season in
order to become rejuvenated.

In the controversial essay "The Historical Roots of Our
Ecological Crisis," Lynn White doesn't take kindly to
evangelicals when it comes to environmentalism. John Calvin
was one of the first to biblically justify the indiscriminate
exploitation of natural resources, White argues. Among other
things, Calvinism teaches that we humans have been given
dominion over nature, and White writes that the reformer's
spiritual descendants have indeed dominated nature with a
vengeance, ruthlessly profiting from—and consequently
exhausting—the resources of creation.

White misunderstands Calvin, who actually taught responsible stewardship in which the blessings of God could be enjoyed for more generations than just one's own. To violate or fall short of this trust, taught Calvin, was sin—and would carry dire consequences.

Case in point: I am convinced that the documented increase in the incidence of cancer today is related to what we have been doing to nature. There is growing evidence, for example, that our use of hydrocarbons has been releasing into the upper atmosphere a variety of chemicals that are depleting the ozone layer, which protects us from the harmful ultraviolet rays of the sun. The diminishing filtering capabilities of the ozone layer means that harmful, cancer-causing rays are getting through to us.

Furthermore, the chemicals increasingly used for fertilizer are invading our bodies via our food. Some of these chemicals pose grave health hazards, carcinogenous and otherwise.

And these are just short-term effects of our environmental irresponsibility. Long-term effects will be endured by our children and grandchildren. The unprecedented amounts of carbon monoxide we are pumping into the atmosphere are forming a gaseous layer girdling the earth that essentially traps the heat generated by the earth, and that would normally dissipate into space. Except that the heat is having a harder and harder time escaping the atmosphere, thanks to the greenhouse effect of the gaseous layer. The cumulative result? A gradual increase in global temperatures, which is already being noticed and documented. Such shifts in global temperatures in turn trigger ominous changes in the earth's climate and weather.

For instance, scientists are discovering that centuries-old polar glaciers are melting at an alarming rate due to global warming—causing some to predict that the additional volume of water will raise ocean levels. This will put coastal areas of continents—along which a large proportion of the world's population lives—under water. As the warming effect continues, areas that are now temperate—again, where most of the world's population live—will become tropical, and tropical areas will tend toward desertification.

Picture what this could look like: our great-grandchildren could end up living in a world in which New York's Hudson River is lined with palm trees…Phoenix has uninterrupted weeks of temperatures over 120…low-lying Asian nations like Bangladesh are hit with torrential rains and rising floods, killing millions of people and driving survivors to higher ground in India and Pakistan…profound climate change triggers massive migrations, with not merely regional but global implications.

The long-term effects of our environmental irresponsibility go beyond climate. What respiratory illnesses will our grandchildren suffer because of our abuse of the atmosphere? How much less aesthetic joy and fulfillment will our descendents know in this world because our rape of the earth's surface is destroying its beauty?

As the environment suffers duress, our capacity to produce enough food for an expanding human family will diminish—and as always happens, the poor suffer most profoundly in a crisis. Deforestation and resulting soil erosion has already reduced the food-production capacities of poor nations like Haiti and Bangladesh, which are sustained only by massive shipments of food. Weather changes caused by the clear-cutting of rain forests are already affecting poor people around the world. If we are to concern ourselves with the needs of the poor, as Jesus has mandated, then we will have to be environmentally concerned.

In Africa I visited a tribal chief whose people lived along the Senegal River south of Mauritania. His nomadic tribe was dying out. A prolonged drought had killed the herds of goats, that for generations had been their livelihood. Young people in growing numbers were leaving tribal life for Dakar, the nearest city, in hope of finding some means of survival. The chief had no doubts that his people were facing extinction.

What can be done? I asked him.

He shrugged. "Nothing," he said. "This is not a drought. We have had droughts before. My people know how to live through droughts. This is the world changing. All the land is turning into desert, and there can be no future for us when that happens."

The chief was not educated in meteorology or geography, but he knew in ways that transcend Western education that something cataclysmic was happening to the environment. This chief did not need to read journal articles about the effect of diminishing rain forests on global weather patterns. He did not need to read studies that trace the expansion of the Sahara Desert southward into the heart of Africa. He did not need to cite statistics, like how the Sahara is moving south at the rate of two miles a year. He just knew, as certainly as any college-trained professional.

If our own destruction of nature diminishes the ability of the earth to yield food, then poor people will starve in greater and greater numbers. At present, according to Compassion International, more than forty thousand children in this world die *daily* from starvation and disease related to malnutrition. How many more will be dying from these causes decades from now?

Christians Should Make Environmentalism a High Priority Because Our Annihilation of Natural Life Impacts the Worship of God.

In our self-centeredness, we are prone to think that only humans have the urge or capacity to worship the Creator. But the Bible is quite clear that *all* of nature—animal, vegetable, and mineral—was created for the worship of God.

Face it—worshiping is important to Western Christians, but not as important as *doing*. We are activists. Even in matters of faith, we are so utilitarian that we have difficulty grasping that praise to God is valuable in and of itself. Ultimately, God created us and saved us to bring honor and glory to himself, not so that we could do things for him. And all of nature was created for this same purpose, too.

> *Praise ye the Lord. Praise ye the Lord from the heavens; praise him in the heights.*
> *Praise ye him, all his angels; praise ye him all his hosts.*
> *Praise ye him, sun and moon: praise him, all ye stars of light.*
> *Praise him, ye heavens of heavens, and ye waters that be above the heavens.*
> *Let them praise the name of the Lord: for he commanded, and they were created.* (Psalm 148:1–5)

Angels, heavens, waters, beasts—each kind of creation reflects God's glory and lifts up praise to him in its own way. With or without what we would call self-consciousness, all created things and beings were ordained to reflect the glory of God and to magnify his name in worship.

I'm an evangelist out to save the whales, a friend teases me. Guilty as charged: yes, my primary obligation as an evangelist is to tell other people about what Jesus had done for them—and I am also obliged to do what Jesus said: save the whales.

One should really follow the other. When a person is saved and filled with the Holy Spirit, there is created in us an impulse to pour out songs and shouts of praise to the Lord—in the words of the old hymn, to "join with all nature in manifold witness" to the glory of our God.

When we understand the ultimate priority of worship, then we can understand why saving the whales—and all other species and forms of life on this earth—is so important. Humpback whales sing songs...flying fish leap from the sea...eagles soar in glorious circles above giant, reverent sequoias...flowers and butterflies splash color across the landscape...the miraculous intricacies and symbioses of plants and insects. God made them all for his glory, each to praise him in its own way.

It is said that Francis of Assisi once called on crickets to chirp music for their Maker, and that he called on the grazing sheep to lift their voices and "baa" unto the Lord. If you call St. Francis crazy, you are making a confession, not accusation. For what you say about such behavior only reveals how far you are removed from saintly spirituality.

If St. Francis were among us today, he would be an environmentalist. He would preach the biblical mandate to rescue nature from its present painful condition. He would remind us that St. Paul has called us to rescue creation so that all of nature could join him in worship. He would ask us to listen to what we sing weekly in the Doxology:

> Praise God, from whom all blessing flow;
> Praise Him, all creatures here below;
> Praise Him above, ye heavenly host;
> Praise Father, Son and Holy Ghost."

"Praise him, all creatures here below." That is why Christian environmentalism is not an oxymoron. Being environmentally concerned is an expression of being Christian.

Like most other aspects of God and Christianity, environmentalism has been twisted away from the truth, has been distorted or misdirected or diluted by New Age emphases, paganism, and politics. Christians must be ready to rescue the truth and return it to the whole counsel of God. Consider these guidelines as you embrace environmentalism:

- *Nature is not to be worshipped.* Nature is not God. God is outside of and other than nature. He holds nature together. Any worship of nature is no more or less than idolatry (see Romans 1:23).

- *Human beings are infinitely more precious to God than all the rest of nature.* In the hierarchy of nature, humans are above all else in God's creation. There is a spirituality to humans that is unique, and it is primarily for our salvation that Christ went to the cross.

- *In this hierarchy of life, there is nothing wrong with sacrificing lower forms of life in order to sustain higher forms of life.* Vegetarianism or veganism may be a good idea, but it is not a biblical mandate for this present age.

Perhaps it is time for all Christians to overcome their fears of being Christian environmentalists and save the earth without worshipping it. Now is the accepted time, today is the day of salvation—not only for our spiritual salvation, but also for the physical salvation of all that is in God's world.

I only wish I had written this chapter. On a good day off you'll find me waist-deep in the Potomac River, casting for smallmouth bass and enjoying the goldfinches and orioles crossing the river overhead. Or thigh-deep in a marsh listening to spring peepers and wood frogs singing, or knee-deep in the summer grasses of a meadow with a song of praise in my heart inspired by the crickets and prairie warblers and song sparrows.

I have, however, a slight quarrel with the three qualifications Tony makes at the chapter's end.

Nature is not to be worshipped, he writes; nature is not God. Of course. God is indeed totally other than nature, in that you could subtract all of creation and God would not be diminished at all. And yes, God is outside of nature, and nature worship is idolatry. Yet I think that God is *in* nature as well as outside of it (God fills all things, Scripture says), that God is totally *with* nature as well as totally other from it (the Incarnation of Jesus demonstrates God's solidarity not only with humanity, but with all of creation), and that nature, while not God, is even more linked to God than an artist's painting or symphony or sculpture is to the artist (God cares for every sparrow, clothes every wildflower, as Jesus says).

I also struggle with Tony's assertion that human beings are infinitely more precious to God than all the rest of nature. The words *infinitely* and *all* are weighty words. I wonder why we tend to emphasize so strongly the difference and distance between humanity and the rest of creation. Personally, I find myself emphasizing humanity as *part of* creation, not *above* it. And I see Christ's work on the cross as saving *all* creation, including but not only humanity. On a very practical level, unless humanity is turned from its destructive path, humanity will destroy creation; so the two—the salvation of humanity and the salvation of the planet (and maybe far beyond, if we extend our capability for interplanetary travel over the next centuries)—seem to me inextricably bound together.

Finally, Tony's statement that there is nothing wrong with sacrificing lower forms of life in order to sustain higher forms of life strikes me as a bit too carte-blanche. I would like to think that Tony meant to say that it *can be justifiable* to sacrifice lower forms of life to sustain higher forms. (Although when it comes to our bodies, don't the microbes win in the end?) The difference between *can be justifiable* and *there is nothing wrong* is the difference between full-color thinking and black-and-white thinking. This difference forces us to ask, "Is this a *justifiable* sacrifice we're asking the planet to make for our benefit? On what grounds?"

As humans become more and more dominant on our planet (think of cities, roads, pollution, global warming, extinctions, monoculture, et cetera), and as more and more supposedly lower forms of life are being sacrificed to sustain us, we will need to ask more and more frequently, "Is there any point at which we need to say that we humans have gone too far, demanded too much, forced other creatures to sacrifice too much on our account? What justifies such an extravagant, ongoing indulgence of one self-centered species at the expense of God's beautiful planet?"

I don't think the point at which these questions must be asked is centuries or decades in front of us: I think we are already well past that point and don't realize it.

MISSING THE POINT:
Homosexuality

Tony Campolo

What critics of my beliefs about homosexuality do not understand is that I'm trying to make up for a horrendous failure
during high school.

Roger was gay, we all knew it, and we all made his life
miserable. When we passed him in the hall, we called out his
name effeminately, we made the crude gestures, we made him the
brunt of cheap jokes. He never took showers in PE, because he
knew we'd whip him with our wet towels.

I wasn't there, though, the day they dragged Roger into the
shower room, and shoved him into the corner. Curled up there,
he cried and begged for mercy as five guys urinated on him.

The reports said that Roger went to bed that night as usual,
and that sometime around two in the morning he got up, went
down to the basement of his house, and hanged himself.

On that day I realized that I wasn't a Christian. I was a
theologically sound evangelical, believed all points of the
Apostle's Creed, declared Jesus to be my Savior. But if the Holy
Spirit had actually been in me, I would have stood up for Roger.
When the guys came to make fun of him, I would have put one
arm around Roger's shoulders, waved the guys off with the other
and told them to leave him alone, to not mess with him, because
he was my friend.

But I was afraid to be Roger's friend. I knew that if you stood
up for a homosexual, people say cruel things about you, too. So I
kept my distance. If I hadn't, who knows if Roger might be alive
today.

I am not asking that Christians gloss over biblical teachings,
nor that we justify same-gender eroticism. I am simply reminding
Christians that we are supposed to love people—even those we
have been socially conditioned to despise. I am calling Christians
to reach out and show kindness and affection toward their
homosexual neighbors—who number at least fifteen million in the
United States. If we Christians cannot love these neighbors as we

love ourselves, then we are violating the command of Jesus (Matthew 19:19) and ought not call ourselves his followers.

I believe that if Jesus were in our shoes, he would reach out in love to his homosexual brothers and sisters and demand that they be treated justly, that we end the discrimination that has too often made homosexuals into second-class citizens and denied them their constitutional rights. If Jesus were in our shoes, he would work to create an atmosphere in society wherein homosexuals could be open about who they are without fear of oppression and persecution. If Jesus were in our shoes, those with a homosexual orientation would be treated with dignity and respect.

It is *very* important to distinguish between a homosexual *orientation* and homosexual *behavior*. Orientation is who a person is; behavior is what a person does. A homosexual orientation is the desire to have sexual intimacy with a person of the same gender. Homosexual behavior is erotic physical interaction between persons of the same gender. The orientation is not chosen; behavior is.

As will be discussed later, I believe the Bible tells us that same-gender eroticism is wrong. So do many Christians I know with a homosexual orientation—Christians who call upon the power of the Holy Spirit to help them say no to their desire for same-sex eroticism. Their desire to gratify their desires with sexual intimacy with persons of their own sex may be constant—just as heterosexual desire can be constant for many—but they are "more than conquerors through Christ who strengthens" them (Romans 8:37).

These are brave saints who endure lives of sexual frustration because of their commitment to what they believe are biblical admonitions against homosexual intercourse. Many such Christians have told me about long nights of spiritual agony as they have struggled against the flesh to remain faithful to what they believe to be the will of God. They fight to remain celibate for the sake of Christ.

Yet a lot of Christians say victory over temptation isn't enough. If homosexuals really want to be saved, they must lose their homosexual *orientation*. Through prayer they should be transformed into heterosexuals. And there is no end of testimonies of homosexuals who have been "healed" of homosexuality and are now leading happy heterosexual lives. They say that what God has done for them, God can and will do for anyone who asks.

I do not argue with the claim that God *can* do anything. After all, God is God. But there is a big difference between what God *can* do and what God *will* do. The former is a doctrine; the latter is a presumption. It is utterly simplistic to believe that just because God *can* do something, he *will* do it—and especially if we beg God to do it.

We all know people who have prayed desperately for something God can do, only to find that for reasons that are incomprehensible, God does not. Countless Christians have prayed for a loved one to be delivered from cancer, only to have that loved one die. Yes, God *could* heal cancer, and he certainly *has* healed cancer in others—but he did *not* heal this person. Dietrich Bonhoeffer prayed for the deliverance of the Jews during the Holocaust, discovering that the God who could deliver them did in fact not deliver them.

I know homosexuals who have prayed desperately, even to exhaustion, to be delivered from their homosexual orientation— but in vain. Yes, I believe that all prayers are eventually answered, some of them in heaven. But at the moment we live in the ugly here-and-now rather than the sweet by-and-by, and a lot of evangelical homosexuals are suffering frustration in spite of their earnest prayers. I do not understand why this is so, but I cannot deny that it is so.

Those who despise homosexuals are often ignorant of what science is discovering. There is a growing body of evidence that, as mentioned earlier, homosexual orientation is not a choice. Some researchers, for instance, argue for a genetic explanation, citing the claim by Dean Hamer that the Xq28 gene is causal for homosexuality. Yet most researchers say that such genome studies are too new and inconclusive to be dependable.

Others point to the findings of a seldom cited physiological study suggesting that sexual orientation in animals is controlled by hormones. Research demonstrates that the disruption of certain hormones at certain stages in the fetal development of rats significantly alters their sexual orientation. Such a disruption can be caused by, among other things, the pregnant mother's trauma or intense nervous tension. This research suggests that normal sexual orientation of males is the result of programming, or "imprinting," the brain with testosterone in the late stages of fetal development—and that trauma in the mother during this stage can interfere with normal imprinting, resulting in the homosexual orientation of her offspring.

There are problems with this theory, of course. It offers little about the causes of lesbianism, for example; what causes homosexual orientation in females may in fact differ from what causes homosexuality in males. Lesbianism seems to spring more from psychosocial influences; male homosexuality, from biophysical influences. John Money, professor and researcher at Johns Hopkins University, suggests a kind of interaction between sociological and biological influences that together create homosexual orientations. And there is growing opinion among researchers that there even may be various subtypes of homosexuals, each with its own specific causes.

I frankly believe that at the present time *nobody* knows what creates homosexual orientations. All the evidence points away from simple, single-cause explanations. But one thing seems clear to me: *homosexual orientations are not chosen.* Whatever the causes, the imprinting of sexual orientation occurs so early in children's biosocial development that they can make no conscious decision about it. Homosexuals do not choose their sexual orientation any more than heterosexuals do. Why would they? Why would anyone deliberately *choose* to be homosexual? The psychological pain and social oppression that many homosexuals live with are hardly the sorts of things one chooses.

Yet among those who claim to have changed from a homosexual to a heterosexual orientation, there seems to be a preponderance of bisexuals. Bisexuality sits right in the middle of the continuum that extends from "pure" heterosexuality to "pure" homosexuality. Bisexuals are sexually attracted to individuals both of the same and the opposite gender. Some bisexuals choose a homosexual lifestyle; others, a heterosexual lifestyle; still others conduct sexual relations with both males and females. A traditional evangelical remedy for bisexuals is to counsel them into a monogamous heterosexual lifestyle, for that not only offers them the best hope for social adjustment given the world in which we live, but also conforms to what I believe to be a biblically prescribed lifestyle.

Counseling bisexuals into heterosexuality, however, is an entirely different matter than counseling true homosexuals into heterosexuality. I believe strongly that homosexuals did not and cannot choose their orientation.

Those who despise homosexuals are ignorant not only of science, but of the Bible's teachings on the subject. Here, for example, are Bible passages often cited as evidence that homosexuality is a sinful choice, along with interpretations of these passages that are not accepted by many evangelicals, but at least deserve serious consideration.

Torah

In Leviticus 18:22, Leviticus 20:13, and Deuteronomy 23:17-18 are harsh prohibitions against, apparently, homosexuality. Yet some scholars contend that these passages do not apply to the modern homosexual argument because these prohibitions are part of the *purity code* of ancient Israel, rather than the *moral code*. The moral code—that is, the Ten Commandments—is binding for all people at all times, whereas the purity code is what we commonly call Kosher rules for Orthodox Jews. The purity code condemns such practices as eating shellfish, wearing fabric that is made out of more than one kind of thread, having sexual intercourse with a woman while she is menstruating, eating pork and even touching the skin of a dead pig. Most Christians (but by no means all) agree that purity codes, or Kosher rules, do not apply to Christians, who are now obligated only to obey the moral laws of Scripture. What had been declared unclean is no longer viewed as such (Acts 10:9-16; Romans 14:14).

(One rabbi informed me, however, that the measure of how seriously a purity rule should be taken is related to the punishment cited for its violation—in the case of homosexual behavior, death. By this gauge, then, one cannot easily discard this rule.)

Gospels

Jesus undoubtedly knew about homosexuality, and we can assume that he held to the teachings of the Torah on the subject. But nowhere does he condemn gays and lesbians. In fact, Jesus never mentions homosexuality even once.

Homosexuality just isn't on his Top Ten list of sins. What *is* number one on that list, however, is judgmental religious people who look for sin in the lives of others without dealing with the sin in their own lives (Matthew 23). Furthermore, it is uncomfortable to note that, although Jesus is silent about homosexuality, he specifically condemns the remarriage of divorced people—a practice accepted by most modern Christians.

Pauline letters: 1 Timothy 1:10-11
"[The law is not made for a righteous man, but]...for whoremongers, for them that defile themselves with mankind, for menstealers, for liars, for perjured persons, and if there be any other thing that is contrary to sound doctrine; according to the glorious gospel of the blessed God, which was committed to my trust." [KJV]

There is considerable opinion among biblical scholars that here in this letter to his protégé Timothy, Paul was condemning not homosexuality per se, but pederasty—which was much more accepted in ancient Greece than it is today. Then a male teacher would take on one young boy and personally tutor him. In such a close relationship, it was not uncommon for the teacher to exploit his position of authority by either seducing the boy or coercing him into sexual relations.

And because in Greek culture the youthful boy was its most erotic sexual object, the farther into puberty the boy progressed, the less attractive he became. When the student was no longer desirable to the teacher, he usually was cast aside for newer and younger sexual partners. So some male students tried to prolong their boyish attractiveness by concealing their oncoming maturity—and assuming effeminate mannerisms was one technique these psychologically and physically abused young men used.

Abandoned sooner or later, these boys were usually left psychologically devastated and often suicidal.

Pederasty was abhorrent to the apostle Paul. He took great offense at all forms of sexual exploitation, and this hideous form of it—so common in ancient Greece—was a particular target of his ire. Yet it is a mistake, say some biblical ethicists, to equate pederasty to a committed, monogamous homosexual relationship chosen in love.

Pauline letters: 1 Corinthians 6:9

"Do you not know that the wicked will not inherit the kingdom of God? Do not be deceived: Neither the sexually immoral nor idolaters nor adulterers nor male prostitutes nor homosexual offenders..."

Yet even here, with the clear mention of the word *homosexual*, the case is nonetheless foggy. The Greek word *arsenokoitai*, translated as *homosexual* in the New International Version, has an ambiguous meaning: the word was seldom used in ancient literature, and so scholars cannot pin down the meaning with any certainty. We know that it refers to some form of condemned sexual behavior, but we don't know specifically that what is being condemned is homosexual behavior as we understand it.

Pauline letters: Romans 1:26-27

"...God gave them over to shameful lusts. Even their women exchanged natural relations for unnatural ones. In the same way the men also abandoned natural relations with women and were inflamed with lust for one another. Men committed indecent acts with other men, and received in themselves the due penalty for their perversion."

One interpretation of this passage is that St. Paul does not condemn those born with homosexual orientations, but rather heterosexuals who, by giving unrestrained vent to their lusts, become debased and decadent. Such scholars contend that the apostle is condemning those who *choose* homosexual behavior as a new, kinky sexual thrill—who adopt homosexuality as perversion.

This interpretation is premised on Paul writing his letter to the Romans while in Corinth, a Greek city whose dominant religion was the worship of Aphrodite. Aphrodite was a hermaphroditic deity whose worshipers—heterosexual men and women—acted as members of the opposite sex to experience the sexual side of their deity that differed from their own. According to this interpretation, in Romans 1 Paul is railing against idolatry and the obscene sexual practices that he was familiar with in Corinth; he was *not* condemning homosexuality per se.

The only problem with these otherwise convincing arguments from biblical interpretation is that Christian tradition has consistently held that St. Paul specifically condemned all homosexual eroticism. Biblical interpretations notwithstanding, to contradict two millennia of church tradition seems a little bit arrogant to me. The church fathers, who were closest to Paul, exemplify this (see Cyprian of Carthage, *Letters 1:8*, and John Chrysotom's *Homily on Romans 1:26-27*).

Yet, point out others, if we yielded to church tradition on *all* points, women would not be allowed to teach Sunday school or serve as missionaries. Furthermore, most of the references in the writings of church fathers to homosexual behavior condemn the exploitation of boys rather than homosexual orientation or committed, loving homosexual marriages. Finally, some point out, what we hear from the early centuries of the church is from only the church fathers, because the church mothers had to keep their mouths shut.

Evangelical homosexuals are torn not only between their sexual orientations and tradition biblical interpretations, but also between the homosexual community—which offers acceptance and companionship—and the straight church, which usually means estrangement and loneliness. Their anguish is seldom appreciated by heterosexuals. Yet there are some solutions to this dilemma of Christian homosexuals.

Two Christian homosexual men I know in Chicago solved their problem of loneliness by entering a covenant wherein they promised to, 1) live with each other "'til death do we part," and 2) do so celibately. They chose to live together as lifelong partners "in all love and tenderness" but without erotically sexual behavior. These two men claimed to be enjoying the humanizing benefits of a genuine love relationship that has given them mutual blessings, but that did not violate biblical admonitions against homosexual intercourse. I have recently learned of a number of other evangelical and homosexual couples who have adopted a similar arrangement.

By the way, I call this a homosexual *covenant* rather than a homosexual *marriage* because of the sexual consummation implied by the latter word. And *covenant* connotes a lifelong commitment of mutual obligation, which does not necessitate sexual intercourse. Such "wedded friendships" were affirmed within the Church of England from the middle ages right up through the mid-17th century, claims Alan Bray of the University of London, who cites an array of specific cases in which these celibate relationships were given church blessings (see *The Tablet*, 4 August 2001, pp. 1108-09).

Many Christians will disapprove of this arrangement, of course, claiming that the Bible frowns on if not outright condemns mere romantic feelings between members of the same sex. The Bible tells us to flee temptation, they point out, and such "wedded friendships" obviously put gays and lesbians in very trying situations.

Yet these hard-line critics are hard-pressed to build a solid biblical case for their complaints. If they say that lovers cannot live in such a relationship without becoming sexually involved, they are making value judgments about the moral strength and integrity of other Christians— judgments of psychological projection more than anything else.

Another answer to the loneliness faced by Christian homosexuals is to live in community. Thousands of Christians across America are finding that it is spiritually and economically beneficial to live together in groups ranging from three or four to ten or more. Such Christian communities can foster high commitment among the members—which, when it comes to sexuality, means that sexual behavior can be more easily held in check, thanks to the loving and prayerful support of others. A Christian community can be a safe place for homosexual persons to be honest about their orientation, so that community members can encourage each other to lifestyles that glorify Christ.

In such communities, being homosexual or heterosexual would not be a watershed issue, but *all* members could use their own gifts from God to help others. And who knows but that, observing Christian communities with members of all sexual orientations, evangelical churches would be challenged to realize that "they" are indeed part of "us," and that we are to be mutually responsible and compassionate.

It is a shame and a sin that persons with homosexual orientation are usually forced to discover and use their gifts *outside* the church. Through their struggles, some of our homosexual brothers and sisters have grown in the Lord to the point where they have much that would benefit and bless the straight church.

There *must* be good news for homosexuals. In the likelihood that their sexual orientations will not change, we must do more than simply bid them to be celibate: we must find ways for them to have fulfilling, loving experiences so that their humanity is affirmed and their participation in the body of Christ is ensured. Homosexuals *are* our brothers and sisters—and they must be treated that way. To do less is sin.

McLaren Responds

What if my child told me, "Dad, I think I'm homosexual"? What if the child of a church friend were homosexual? How would I want the church to respond to my child?

This isn't a theoretical question. Tony's chapter helps people translate this from an abstract question for theologians, or from a political question for the Religious Right, into a very practical and personal issue for all of us: *How do we treat our neighbors, our colleagues, our sons and daughters?* Before focusing on the morality of "their" sexual partners, Tony forces us to face the morality of *our* treatment of fellow human beings, neighbors, people Jesus loves and to whom Jesus sends us to express that love.

This issue ceased being theoretical for me a few years ago, when I made the very worst mistake of my pastoral career. Our church has a listserv where members dialogue about faith issues. For a few weeks homosexuality was the subject of a lively discussion. A man in our church who had struggled with homosexual orientation for his entire adult life, and who had confided his struggles to me, wanted to post a message so that others could know what a homosexual feels like when he hears statements like "Hate the sin, love the sinner." But he couldn't break his anonymity: that would be too risky and painful for him and his family. So to preserve his anonymity, he asked me to post his message under the pseudonym *Pain*.

He sent me the message to post, and I did. What I didn't realize was that, when I copied his message, I also copied the return-path information at the bottom of his e-mail. Anyone who read his e-mail to the end could read his name. I had no idea what I had done until a friend called me and told me. Mortified, I called the man, who had already seen my mistake. I rushed to his house, where I found him weeping. His wife was weeping.

I died inside. But we talked, we prayed, I apologized, he forgave me.

Still, the fact remains that a homosexual man whom I had hurt so deeply (though accidentally) was far more merciful to me than most of our churches are to homosexuals.

SOUL

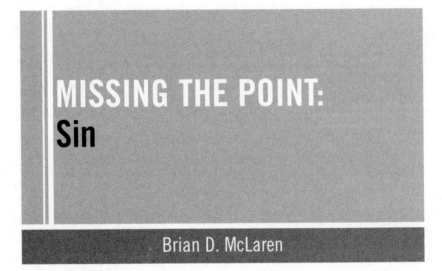

MISSING THE POINT:
Sin

Brian D. McLaren

In the early fifth century Augustine was bishop of Hippo in North Africa (modern-day Algeria) Among his duties was the oversight of the monks and priests in his area. When a monk and a priest in his charge became involved in a homosexual relationship, Augustine confronted what was viewed as unacceptable behavior for Christians, not to mention for supposed celibates. Then, in a sermon to his congregation, Augustine spoke directly to the incident, which had become public. In his sermon he defused the temptation to gossip and judge, using a Pauline passage to do it:

> *Besides everything else, I face daily the pressure of my concern for all the churches. Who is weak, and I do not feel weak? Who is led into sin, and I do not inwardly burn?* (2 Corinthians 11:28)

Augustine's handling of this delicate matter resonates with something I experience in my pastoral ministry and my Christian life. It is a constant quandary, a choice I must make again and again, a question I must answer daily: *How will I respond to the faults and failings and sins of my sister and brother Christians?* With superiority and condemnation? With condoning and toleration? Or with something better, something redemptive, something like compassion and humility?

I am sorry to say that, at first blush, I find Augustine's response (like Paul's before him) distasteful. I'd rather distance myself from others in their failures; instead I am invited to identify with them. They demonstrate personal or moral or ethical or spiritual weakness, and I am told to feel weak with them. They do wrong, and my face burns red with a shared shame.

The commanded response is charitable, no doubt. But it is more than charitable: it is honest and realistic. John Donne's words "Ask not for whom the bell tolls; it tolls for thee" could be adapted "Ask not how someone could be so weak: the same weakness is in you." Which is essentially what Paul had in mind when he wrote,

If you think you are standing firm, be careful that you don't fall. No temptation has seized you except what is common to man.
(1 Corinthians 10:12-13)

So the failures of others remind me of this: I also am temptable. I also can fall. I also am weak.

I've been thinking about weakness a lot lately. I've been thinking how often I am not strong, not successful, not together, not "victorious," but instead how I am weak, just barely surviving, how easily and fast I could fall. And lately I've been appreciating the virtue of simply surviving.

This hit me strongly when I spent the day at the hospital with my son. Nothing too serious: he had fractured his thumb playing lacrosse and needed some pins inserted so the bones would align and heal correctly. It was an outpatient procedure, minor surgery—in and out in six hours.

But it was an intense day for me. Twelve years earlier I had been in a hospital with Trevor, that time because he had been diagnosed with leukemia. Then he was just six years old, maybe 40 pounds. Now he was a strapping six-foot-one, 190 pounds, driving, shaving, answering his own questions for the doctor. He was a leukemia survivor.

After the hand surgery—groggy from the anesthesia, his hand in a monster of a cast—Trevor couldn't button or zip his pants or get his own shoes on. As I helped him dress himself, it was just like a dozen years earlier, helping my little guy dress after a surgery that had installed a pair of mainline catheter ports in him. I wheeled him out to the car just like the last time, my son the leukemia survivor.

So you can imagine how precious that word *survivor* is to me. The word describes me, too—all of us, in fact: Christians, leaders, pastors. We're not that strong. We're not that successful. At best, we're all just survivors. Like Trevor, we've got some amazing stories to tell, some scars to show for our survival.

Most pastors know all about surviving. Only a pastor truly understands what it feels like to have yet another person call to tell you they're leaving the church—a person you love, a person you helped and served, a person who needed you, a person you feel you now need, and yet the person is going, leaving, abandoning, rejecting. You know the talk: "You're not feeding us, pastor...I'm going somewhere where I can get more meat, not just milk." People go, and they take a chunk of your heart with them. And of your morale. And with them goes some of your naivete. Somehow you survive. Sometimes just by a fingernail, sometimes weak, usually scarred. But you survive.

Only a pastor truly understands what it feels like to fire someone you have discipled, someone you trained and encouraged and then brought onto your staff, but who didn't last, no matter how much you tried to help them. Then the ex-staffer feels you turned on them, betrayed them, and soon members of your congregation assume the same. And you play it over and over in your mind, and you can't imagine how you could have done any better. But that knowledge doesn't keep you from feeling miserable and weak, not just for a week or two, but for months.

But you survive.

The anguish of losing your faith is particularly excruciating when you're a pastor. Too many unanswered prayers, yours and your people's. Too many deacons who are publicly righteous and biblical, and only you know how mean-spirited and small-minded they are. Too many sermons that didn't make that big a difference, in spite of your prayers and tears and painstaking preparations. Too few thank-yous, too few breakthroughs. Too many arguments with your wife or fights with your kids or lustful thoughts (way too many of those). And you feel that the words that are supposed to be honey in your mouth and fire in your bones become dust in your mouth and weariness in your bones. Yet Sundays relentlessly roll around every seven days, and you wonder how long you will last, and your wife wants you to see a counselor because she thinks you're clinically depressed. And who knows what your elders are thinking. And you know what *you're* thinking: you aren't strong. You aren't successful. You are weak, barely surviving.

But you survive.

In 2 Corinthians 1:8–10 the apostle Paul writes:

> *We do not want you to be uninformed, brothers, about the hardships we suffered in the province of Asia. We were under great pressure, far beyond our ability to endure, so that we despaired even of life. Indeed, in our hearts we felt the sentence of death. But this happened that we might not rely on ourselves but on God, who raises the dead. He has delivered us from such a deadly peril, and he will deliver us. On him we have set our hope that he will continue to deliver us.*

In other words, Paul says, "I was weak, but I survived."

I remember Trevor's days 12 years ago—constant hospital visits, sleepless nights, anguished prayers, painful spinal taps, bone marrow aspirations, nightmarish side effects from drugs, weakness upon weakness. Yet Trevor survived. And so did we.

I remember the two or three years I spent not that long ago: preaching every week, but wondering whether my own faith would survive. It did. And now I identify with other of Paul's words from that same letter:

> *But we have this treasure in jars of clay to show that this all-surpassing power is from God and not from us. We are hard pressed on every side, but not crushed; perplexed, but not in despair; persecuted, but not abandoned; struck down, but not destroyed. We always carry around in our body the death of Jesus, so that the life of Jesus may also be revealed in our body. For we who are alive are always being given over to death for Jesus' sake, so that his life may be revealed in our mortal body....*
>
> *Therefore we do not lose heart. Though outwardly we are wasting*

away, yet inwardly we are being renewed day by day. For our light and momentary troubles are achieving for us an eternal glory that far outweighs them all. So we fix our eyes not on what is seen, but on what is unseen. For what is seen is temporary, but what is unseen is eternal.
(2 Corinthians 4:7-11, 16-18)

Pressed, perplexed, persecuted, abandoned—it's amazing what we survive, as weak as we are. And it is also amazing to look back and think, *I have been renewed day by day. I'm back. I survived.*

Whatever siege or nightmare or failure you're going through now, try to imagine this: someday you'll be looking back, 12 years will have passed, and you will have survived. You're a survivor.

And when you see others struggling and stumbling and falling, don't distance yourself from them or their weakness. Don't miss the point by condemning them. Empathize instead. Draw close. Like Augustine, identify with your weak brother or sister, because you're no different. And believe that just as you have by grace survived "many dangers, toils, and snares," they can survive, too. For we serve a God who says, "My power is made perfect in weakness" (2 Corinthians 12:8).

It has been said that you'll never know that Jesus is all there is until Jesus is all you've got—a state of affairs that often accompanies failure, moral and otherwise.

A decade or so ago, when television evangelists right and left seemed to be falling by the wayside, I spoke at a denominational meeting of mainline pastors. Before I was on, the master of ceremonies said something like this to the audience: "We must distance ourselves from the likes of Jim Bakker. Men like this have disgraced the church, and we must make it clear to our people that we are not like that."

His words infuriated me, which explains why I started with words to this effect: "The difference between Jim Bakker and the rest of us is that they haven't found out about the rest of us yet. This is no time to distance ourselves from Jim Bakker, but to acknowledge that what was in him is in us all. The line that separates good from evil does not separate one group of people from another, but runs right down the middle of each of us. Each of us has a dark side—and if the truth were known, each of us would have to run away and hide."

I am not suggesting that we are all adulterers, liars, and embezzlers. All I'm saying is that there is enough evil in the best of us and enough good in the worst of us that it behooves us to not look down on others.

What I wanted to see in this chapter of Brian's, and what I couldn't find, was the reminder that—although we are not sinless—we should sin less. Each of us should be able to say, "While I'm not what I should be, I certainly am not what I was." Each of us should be pressing "toward the mark of the high calling of God and Christ Jesus our Lord" (Philippians 3:13-14).

Granted, we should not measure ourselves against others—but we *should* be taking stock of ourselves continually to see whether or not there is some growth in us, so that we are growing stronger and we are sensing some positive moral transformation in our lives as days go by.

A woman once told me that I wasn't much of a Christian because she knew non-Christians who lived better lives than I did. If those people are so wonderful without Jesus, I asked her, could she imagine how much more wonderful they would be *with* Jesus? And, I added, if I was as rotten as she suspected I was with Jesus, could she imagine what I would be like *without* him?

We must escape the kind of comparisons that Brian so rightly and ably condemns—comparisons wherein we deem ourselves better than others. What Christ has done in my own life does not make me a better Christian than you are, but it does make me a better Christian than I was. And yet there is still my dark side. When I am honest with myself and take a good long look at my dark side, I can find no basis for condemning others.

And more: not only am I not to condemn others in their fallings and failures, but I am to suffer with and weep with those fallen brothers and sisters. For in a very real sense, what happens to one happens to us all. In Galatians 6:1-2 the apostle reminds us that when anyone is overtaken with fault, we must work toward restoration—keeping an eye on ourselves, knowing that somewhere down the line each of us will need restoration, too.

MISSING THE POINT:
Worship

Brian D. McLaren

For the last few years, I have spoken with a lot of young emerging leaders in a lot of different places. Which means I've observed and listened to and worshiped with many dozens of worship bands and worship leaders. Along with the many encouraging trends in worship leading, I have a few persistent concerns about how we may be missing the point about worship.

As a musician as well as a worshiper, I have a great desire to see the music of today reach new heights and new depths to enrich the worship of churches around the world—especially if, as I believe, we are entering (or are well into) a significant period of theological, cultural, and spiritual transition. Perhaps as significant an era as the Reformation itself. If this is true, we should expect to see now—just as was seen during the Reformation—a revitalizing of theology and liturgy that in the end will help us become more biblical, more spiritual, and more effective in our mission.

But here's the rub. In the modern world, theology was articulated by scholars in books and lectures. To the contrary, in the emerging culture it may well be that theologians will leave the library more often and do their research and study among the rest of us. And the best of the emerging theologians will join hands and hearts with poets, musicians, filmmakers, actors, architects, interior designers, landscape designers, dancers, sculptors, painters, novelists, photographers, Web designers—not only to *communicate* an authentically Christian theology for these times, but also to discern it, discover it.

Such a marriage of theologians with artists reflects a shift from left-brain to whole-brain—from reductionist, analytic rationalism to a broader theological holism. The coming theology is one that works in mind *and* heart, understanding *and* imagination, proposition *and* image, clarity *and* mystery, explanation *and* narrative, exposition *and* artistic expression.

And our songwriters and worship leaders could play a huge role in this shift, as they articulate a holistic theology rooted in their own people.

Yet as I sit in scores of venues listening to and participating in extended worship times across the country, I sense that our song lyrics and "worship sets" are too seldom leading us into this new territory. Instead, they effectively take us back to the same old place again and again: a good place, a nice place to visit, but not the right place for Christians to live.

For starters, too many of our lyrics are embarrassingly personalistic, all about Jesus and me. Just listen to the lyrics at your next worship service, and you'll probably hear all about how Jesus forgives me, embraces me, makes me feel his presence, strengthens me, forgives me, holds me close, touches me, revives me, et cetera.

Not that any of this is untrue. Granted, personal intimacy with God is a wonderful step above an abstract, wooden recitation of dogma. But personal intimacy with God isn't the *whole* story. In the emerging culture, in fact, the idea of personal relationship with God isn't necessarily the main point of the story.

If a Martian extraterrestrial were to observe us Westerners worship, I would wager that it would conclude one of the following:

- That we are all mildly dysfunctional and need a lot of hug therapy—ironic, because we are among the most affluent in the world, having been blessed in every way more than any group in history.

- That we don't give a rip about the rest of the world— that our religion makes us spiritually egoistic and selfish.

Not that we are either of these, only that one could easily *conclude* it from observing our worship services. But I *do* believe that we songwriters keep writing songs that reinforce such conclusions because we think that's what people want and need.

So if spiritual songwriting is not primarily about leading people into a deep and personal intimacy with God, what *should* songwriting be about?

I think we would do well to explore these five biblical themes in our lyrics—not to *replace* the idea of personal intimacy, but to add to it, to balance that theme within a broader, bigger picture.

Eschatology

I don't mean putting an apocalyptic novel to music. I mean the biblical vision of God's future which is pulling us toward itself. Many of you, raised like me in late-modern eschatologies, will be surprised to hear that there is a whole new approach to eschatology emerging (led by theologians like Walter Brueggeman, Jürgen Moltmann, Stanley Grenz, and the other "theologians of hope"). This approach doesn't indulge in charts or predictions, but rather bathes itself in the biblical poetry of Isaiah, Jeremiah, Revelation—poetry that, when it enters us, plants in us a vision of a world very much different from and better than ours. And when this hope grows and takes root in us, we become agents of it. Who will write songs expressing the joy captured in Isaiah 9:2-7, Isaiah 25:6-9, Isaiah 35:1-10, or Isaiah 58:5-14?

These songs need to be written because people need hope. People need a vision of a good future. Our imagination needs images that celebrate peace, justice, and wholeness towards which our dismal, conflicted, polluted, and fragmented world is moving. As you can see, this is much bigger than songs about *me* being in *heaven*, bigger than clouds and ethereal imagery.

Songwriters, dig into those poetic passages, and let your heart be inspired to write songs of hope, songs of vision, songs that lodge in our hearts a dream of the future that has been too long forgotten—the dream of God's kingdom coming in justice and compassion and liberation and peace. Of God's will being done *on earth as it is in heaven.*

Mission

As we move into the postmodern world, many believe that worship songwriting needs a new, larger sense of mission—not just missions, not just evangelism—but *mission.* As in participating in the mission of God, the kingdom of God, which is so much bigger and grander than our little schemes of organizational self-aggrandizement.

This strikes at the heart of our consumeristic culture, which is all about me, me, me. The heart of our identity as the church in the new emerging theology is not merely or even primarily that we are blessed, saved, and rescued—which is actually a half-truth heresy that our songs are spreading among our people, albeit inadvertently. Jesus came not to be served, but to serve—which should also be our mission as his followers. Our identity as the church in the new emerging theology— drawing from a fresh reading of Scripture—is that we are the people who, like Abraham, have been blessed *in order to be a blessing.* We are blessed so that we may convey blessing to the world.

Yet for too many of us, the world exists for the church. The world is like a mountain waiting to be strip-mined for converts that will build up the church. Or so the modern church has believed. In the new emerging theology and spirituality, however, this strip-mining approach only mirrors the literal raping and plundering of the environment by modern industrial enterprises: the church becomes just another industry, taking for its own profit, caring little about what kind of mess it leaves behind.

How different is the image of the church as the apostolic community, sent into the world as Christ's hands, feet, eyes, smile, heart. How different is an understanding of a church that exists *for the good of the world*, sent by Jesus as Jesus was sent by the Father.

We need songs that celebrate this missional dimension— good songs, and many. For inspiration we can return to the prophets and the Gospels, engaging the heart of these Scriptures for the poor, the needy, the broken. And why shouldn't these themes be expressed in song? Don't they deserve that dignity?

Historic Christian Spirituality

When we look at the repetitive and formulaic lyrics that millions of Christians are singing (because that's what worship songwriters are writing), the missed opportunities are heartbreaking. As Robert Webber, Thomas Oden, Sally Morgenthaler, and others are teaching us, there is a wealth of historic spiritual writings and prayers that are crying for translation into contemporary song. Every era in history has rich resources to offer—Patristic, Celtic, Puritan periods, and everything in between. On every page of Thomas à Kempis, in every prayer of the great medieval saints, there is inspiration waiting for us, begging to be written into our worship music.

Just God

We also need songs that are simply about God—songs that give God the spotlight just because God is God. Not for the great job God is doing at making me feel warm, loved, tingly, or good. But just because of the character and glory of God. And similarly we need songs that celebrate what God does for the whole world, not just for me or us.

Read the Psalms: they love to celebrate what the Lord does for the *whole earth*, not just the people of Israel. Likewise, we need many songs that celebrate God as Creator—an important theme in Scripture, though unfortunately not in most churches. Because we have lacked a good creation theology in the modern era, we now need theologians to join songwriters and other artists of the emerging culture to celebrate God as God of creation—not only creation at the beginning (whenever that was), but now too: the God who knows the sparrows that fall, whose glory still flashes in the lightning bolt, whose kindness still falls like the morning dew, whose mysteries are still imaged in the depths of the ocean and the vast expanse of the night sky.

Lament

The Bible is full of songs that wail the blues—songs that express the agonizing distance between what we hope for and what we have, what we could be and what we are, what we believe and what we see and feel. The honesty of laments is disturbing, and they seldom end with a Hallmark cliché that fixes the pain. In laments we feel the pain of the chronically ill, the desperately poor, the mentally ill, the lonely, the aged, the forgotten, the oppressed minority, the widow, the orphan.

This pain needs to find its way into songs, and these songs into our churches. The bitter will make the sweet taste even sweeter; and without the bitter, the sweet tastes cloying—and too many of our churches, I venture to guess, already taste like Candyland.

Doesn't our singing endlessly about celebration lose its vitality—and even its credibility—if we don't also sing about the struggle? Is it too much to ask that we be more honest about the pain, disappointment, doubt, and abandonment that is part of our lives? Shouldn't these laments be reflected in the songs of our communities?

A percussive question

Finally, am I the only one wishing for more rhythmic variety? Why is it that I am being blessed so much by creative drummers and percussionists wherever I go—musicians who push the edges rather than remain safe in the white-bread, middle-aged, easy-listening center?

...and about the lyrics of worship music...

Allow me to pose some questions that I've been musing over—not to be critical, but helpful—and to offer ways in which you, with your gifts, can better serve the church and our mission in these transitional times.

- Is it perhaps time to fully and finally get over King James English in our new lyrics, even if we choose to retain it in our old? Enough said.

- Ought we be careful about using gratuitous biblical language—Zion, go forth, on high, et cetera? If there is a good reason to use such language—in other words, if we are using it intentionally, not just for a spiritual feel—then fine. Otherwise, if we can find contemporary language and imagery that communicates more crisply, poignantly, immediately, and deeply to people who have little pew time—then let's use it, in the spirit of 1 Corinthians 14, where intelligibility to the spiritual seeker is a gospel virtue.

- In an era of Columbine and terrorism, does it make sense for us to be more careful about the language of holy war and jihad? I suppose there is a time and place for that, but I don't think this is it. In my opinion, we all need a strong dose of Anabaptist peace right about now.

• Can our worship leaders enrich the musical experience by reading Scripture, great prayers of the historic church, creeds, confessions, and poems over musical backgrounds? Although you may not appreciate the genre, rap music is telling us something about the abiding power of words spoken over music.

• Can the lyricists of our worship music start reading more good poetry, more good prose, so they can be sensitized to the powers of language, the grace of a well-turned phrase, the delight of a freshly discovered image, the prick or punch or caress or jolt that is possible if we wrestle a little harder and stretch a little farther for the word that really wants to be said from deep within us? I feel bad that, while the music of our worship songs is improving, the lyrics can still feel like a cliché train—one linked to another, the plastic language and paper triteness recycled from verse to verse, song to song.

Isn't our God, our mission, our community worthy of more lyrical quality than we are offering so far?

Worship leadership that fails to explore new territory (but rather dispenses products designed in an industry that has as its unspoken aim to deliver a good feeling 52 times a year) can inadvertently lead us not into worship but into temptation. And that's missing the point.

I think worship is a lot like what researchers are discovering about sexuality. Scientists cited in a PBS production on evolution the biological basis of infatuation: the brain seems to be wired to release all kinds of pleasurable brain-bathing chemicals in response to romantic and sexual involvement with an especially attractive object of one's desire. These chemicals make the brain experience a combination of euphoria, obsession, and desire—essential feelings to the procreation of our species. Under the influence of this chemical cocktail in our brains, we are stimulated to make changes in our lives we would never otherwise make—leave father and mother, get a better job, discover the joys of personal grooming, become at least slightly less self-absorbed. (In *The Road Less Traveled: A New Psychology of Love, Traditional Values and Spiritual Growth*, M. Scott Peck describes infatuation as a state of temporary insanity that must be strong enough and last long enough to trick us into making commitments we'd never make in our right minds.)

But just as essential to the survival of the species is an *end* to infatuation. The effect of these chemicals gradually wear off, the scientist explains, so that the couple can settle in and get on with life and responsibly raise any children conceived through their passion. Passion and obsession and euphoria must give way to hard work and nurture and responsibility, said the scientist.

A problem is created when a person becomes addicted to the euphoria of infatuation: when it begins wearing off, they lose interest in their partner and move on to another partner, seeking an encore infatuation experience—which, again, inevitably fades. Such persons mistake the inevitably fading euphoria with a malfunctioning relationship, so they regularly short-circuit the intended process (infatuation, bonding, commitment, responsibility, nurture, childrearing) by moving on to find another high. The addiction that ensues, the scientist said, is every bit as addictive as crack, heroin, alcohol—and perhaps as destructive as well.

So what does all this sex study have to do with worship? Just this: I wonder how many of us develop a kind of addiction to a

211

spiritual feeling, a spiritual infatuation with God, a beautiful thing, a needful thing, but a thing that is not the real point? And I wonder if we worship leaders don't become enmeshed in this addiction—the unwitting codependents of people addicted to spiritual infatuation, dealers in a kind of high.

I know in my city, there are floating congregations of Christians who migrate from church to church; wherever the biggest bang is being felt is where they'll be. They have Christian words for it—"the anointing," perhaps, or "intimacy with God" or "being in the presence of God"—but sometimes I secretly wonder if they have become spiritual infatuation addicts. Whose sermons give them The Feeling? Which worship leader, which songs, which instruments, which vocalists help them get It? Which order of service, how many songs in which order, which combination of high and low volumes or of lentos and allegrettos, which pattern of emotional journey will help people feel The Feeling?

Sometimes I wonder if too many of us assume that The Feeling is the whole point of worship—worse, that it's the whole point of Christianity.

Hold on, you say: what could be better than intimacy with God, or deep worship, or being in God's presence, or experiencing God (phrases commonly used to describe The Feeling)?

My first impulse is to answer you, "Nothing could be better!" Yet in the back of my head I hear a small voice murmuring, *Well, there's always obedience...and service...and faithfulness and humility...* Yet I am not always sure whose voice it is I'm hearing, the Lord's or my own.

At least I know this: in my many years of planning and leading worship services, I have become convinced that God is not as concerned about The Feeling as we are. In fact, God seems sometimes to be downright disrespectful of it. After all, if it were that important, he could stop the baby from crying or the overhead bulb from blowing or the guitar string from breaking or the stomach cramps from starting or the fire alarm from sounding at the worst possible moment. He could answer our prayers (which are prayed with all the fervency of an alcoholic praying for a drink) more faithfully, so that our worship services would deliver The Feeling in ever more consistent and powerful ways.

Experience has made me doubt that God is as concerned about The Feeling as we are. I have come to believe that worship, like sex, involves phases. Yes, infatuations are wonderful. Yes, the ecstasy and euphoria are a wonderful gift that I have enjoyed far more than I deserve. But worship and discipleship are no more about The Feeling than marriage and parenthood and adulthood are about endlessly preserving the brain-cocktail of euphoria.

Yes, I have often stood in worship and prayed or thought, *It's not happening, Lord! Come, Holy Spirit! Make your presence known!* And if I could discern any answering voice at all, all it said was, *Sorry, but no. That's not what you and I are all about right now. I have other things for you. Yes, praise me. Yes, worship me—but not to hype yourself into an all-about-you euphoria.*

And I often hear this question as well: *If you never felt The Feeling again, would you keep worshipping me anyway—for me, and not just for the feeling?*

If you are a worship leader, who will inevitably face these questions, and with them this choice: when parishioners start coming up after service, or sending you emails or anonymous notes ("I really haven't felt the anointing here like I used to...I think the Spirit has departed from our worship...I wish we worshipped like they do down in Jonesville")—when you start getting these responses, you the caring and sincere worship leader will wonder, *Is it my fault? Am I failing God and this congregation? What can I do?*

And so the next week, you may be tempted to resort to hype. You know what it's like—you start to push a little, fake and inflate your emotions a little. You'll act more passionate than you really are, you'll push harder than you should, maybe use a little guilt to get people singing or shouting a little louder. Nothing wrong with that, right? Except that it's a fine line between actor, faker, inflator—and hypocrite. And if you successfully resist that temptation, you will be tempted by something else: depression, discouragement, self-recrimination.

But take heart! It may not be your fault—maybe the lack of The Feeling is actually a wonderful gift, a saving grace, a needed interlude so that you and your congregation don't become infatuation addicts. Maybe the lack of The Feeling is a needed "no" from God so that you'll move on from infatuation to some other things—like obedience, humility, endurance, service, maturity.

Maybe spiritual infatuation with God is missing the point—a near miss, perhaps, but still a miss. Maybe public worship is about more than achieving The Feeling. Maybe public worship is intended to be a runway or launching pad, to inspire us to rise toward a more holistic kind of worship that expresses itself through the lyric of daily living, through the rhythm of work and family and rest and play, through the music of kindness to strangers and labors for justice and deeds of neighborly compassion. Maybe the best worship is what happens after the service, not during it. Maybe the most inspiring worship is that which inspires us to live well after the amplifiers are unplugged.

Campolo Responds

What Brian says about Christian music and its shortcomings seems right on target. His claim that artists rather than scholars will be providing the impulses for the theology of the future provides him with a good reason to call for correctives in the themes that Christian artists communicate in their work. We really do need better eschatology in the songs we sing, that give us hope for the future. Yes, we do need music that gives voice to the mission in the world to which God has called us.

Yet I have a sense that Brian's concept of worship was too concentrated on music. Music is a part of worship, but as I read the chapter it seemed like he made it out to be the totality of worship.

First of all, worship needs to be defined; and furthermore, I believe that this definition should include the idea that worship is something offered up to God. With Kierkegaard I contend that in the worship service, leaders (song leader, worship leader, pastor, choir, organist, et cetera) are the prompters, the congregation are the performers, and God is the audience. In most church services, unfortunately, God is relegated to prompter, the service leaders function as performers, and the congregation is the audience.

Second, I hope that Brian's idea of worship is broader than the single musical issue that he explores, I admit, so thoroughly. As I'm sure Brian would agree, holistic worship involves not only music, but prayers, responsive readings, Scripture, and offering. Worship requires adoration, confession of sin, supplication, and petitions, climaxing with dedications.

A great deal of Christian music is didactic rather than worship-ful—hymns like "My Hope is Built on Nothing Less," "Onward, Christian Soldiers," and "Give of Your Best to the Master." These kinds of hymns carry strong exhortations. These are the hymns that congregations are singing when the song leader interrupts the singing to say, "Read the words! Get the message!" In short, a lot of hymns are simply sermons set to music.

On the other hand, genuine hymns of worship are sung to God, not back at the singers themselves. God is the audience as congregations sing songs of adoration and worship such as "All Glory, Laud, and Honor," "Holy, Holy, Holy," and "Shine, Jesus, Shine."

Finally, what Brian had to say about feelings of infatuation in worship needs further reflection. I'll go him one better: there is nothing wrong, I believe, not only with infatuation, but even with eroticism in worship. St. Teresa's ecstatic outbursts of worship to God were deeply tinged with eroticism. The English metaphysical poet John Donne employed erotic language in his "In Glory to God."

Maybe one of our problems today is that the only kind of eroticism we know is genital eroticism. In earlier times it was not so confined; worship then offered a variety of erotic involvements with God, often through nature and *koinonia*—the latter being that special involvement that Christian people can have with each other in the context of worship and other forms of spiritual fellowship. Which is exactly what sociologist Max Schmolenbach is getting at when he defines true worship as shared ecstasy in which people are caught up in an erotically tinged euphoria wherein they lose their individuality and find a oneness with God and with each other.

MISSING THE POINT:
Doubt

Brian D. McLaren

Doubt. It's like a spiritual drought, a starless night of the soul, a low tide when faith seems to have retreated forever. Nearly all of us experience these dry, dark, difficult times when God doesn't seem real and it's hard to keep going, much less growing. Sometimes these low tides of faith are connected with events: the death of a loved one, a broken relationship, the loss of a job, a prolonged illness, questions raised by a book or a professor. But sometimes they seem to come out of nowhere—it's sunny and bright outside, but inside you feel dark, cloudy, gray, empty.

As a pastor I deal with matters of faith and doubt on a daily basis. And not just other people's faith struggles, either—I experience my own high and low tides of faith even in the midst of an active ministry. Through it all I have learned that doubt can be a doorway to spiritual growth. To flee temptation is our duty as Christians; yet I believe that to flee doubt may lead us to miss the point.

Back when I was a college instructor, I was struck by how superficial many of our Christian answers are in light of the profound questions being asked. And ever since, I have wanted to help Christians have a deeper, more thoughtful faith—and to help spiritual seekers get good answers to their probing questions to help them come to a faith that is honest, vibrant, and growing.

My congregation is composed of people who are generally new to a committed Christian faith. And one of the distinctives of this demographic, I have discovered, is that they haven't yet learned how to be spiritually dishonest. After a service one Sunday, a woman—a growing Christian for several years now—asked me to pray for her. "I'm going through one of those stages again when I don't believe that God exists," she said frankly.

219

The redemptive irony of her request is exquisite: her asking for prayer demonstrated a faith that coexisted with her expressed doubt. Although such a doubt is hardly rare among Christians, her honesty was exceedingly rare.

When committed Christians want to talk about their doubts with me, I tell them this first: doubt is not always bad. In fact, sometimes doubt is absolutely essential. Doubt is like pain: it tells us that something nearby or within us is dangerous. It calls for attention and action.

Doubt is not *always* a virtue, however. There is a dark doubt, an exaggerated and self-destructive doubt that leads to despair, depression, and spiritual self-sabotage. Imagination, for example, is good in itself, but out of control it becomes schizophrenia. Fear is healthy, but out of control fear becomes paranoia. Sensitivity is a wonderful gift, and anger is a necessary emotion—but either one out of control can lead to depression.

Doubt is the same way. Out of control, it becomes unbelief, a hard heart, an arrogant or defeatist cynicism. But healthy doubt can serve as a Geiger counter that detects error. Without it, we'd be gullible, naïve, and just plain stupid (not exactly stellar spiritual qualities). Doubt is similar to guilt, which the late Christian philosopher Francis Schaeffer said was like a watchdog: useful to have around to alert you to danger. But if the watchdog turns and attacks the homeowner, it needs to be restrained and retrained.

So is doubt good or bad? To which I have to answer, yes. It can go either way. Frederick Buechner expresses this ambivalence about doubt beautifully in *Wishful Thinking*: "Whether your faith is that there is a God or that there is not a God, if you don't have any doubts you are either kidding yourself or asleep. Doubts are the ants in the pants of faith. They keep it awake and moving."

Being awake and moving is simply spiritual growth, to which Christians claim to be committed. Spiritual growth means that five years from now, your set of beliefs will hopefully be different from today's—that your beliefs will be more fine-tuned, more tested, more balanced, more examined. And what causes you to examine a belief and test it—against the whole background of Scripture, against the wise thinking of the Christian community at large (both now and through history), against the realities of your experience? Basically, doubt. Whatever inside you that isn't at rest about a belief, that causes you to question that belief. By doubting a belief and then examining it, you can decide to discard it, adjust it, or keep it just as it is.

This is a very different approach to doubt than what I was taught as a boy. The Christianity I grew up with, for instance, perceived science as an enemy. To be a good Sunday school boy, it was required of me to believe that the earth was very young, that the whole fossil record was a hoax, and that biologists and archeologists were conspiring against God—all of which I believed.

Until high school, that is, at which time doubt overcame me. The scientific evidence against my inherited belief system seemed so strong. Thanks to the fact that I was given the freedom to think and read and question my way through doubt, I came to see that my problem wasn't with what the Bible said, but with what some Christians *said* the Bible said. So now I feel free to question church dogma *and* scientific dogma, because I believe that God wants me to seek the truth. And also because anybody—even preachers and scientists alike—can be wrong. I assume that I'm wrong about hundreds of my beliefs, and I hope that God will keep leading me to doubt those beliefs so I can embrace better ones.

But, some point out, won't that openness to doubt lead to spiritual instability and insecurity? Let me ask the opposite question: won't an unwillingness to question lead to a false security that could be even *more* dangerous?

Imagine it's 1860, you're a caucasian Christian in the American South, and your church teaches you that dark-skinned people are inferior and therefore should be slaves to their white superiors. The Bible is cited to buttress this belief as a moral absolute, and to doubt it is treason not only against the state, but against the church, too. Wouldn't you agree that a person would be a better Christian for doubting that belief?

Or take Galileo, who in the 16th century doubted the church's teaching that the sun was in orbit around the earth—which the Bible proved, it was widely believed. Would he have been a better Christian or a better astronomer if he had refused to doubt? Or Martin Luther, who doubted that indulgences had any spiritual legitimacy...or St. Francis or St. Anthony, who doubted that affluence and Christian faith were allies, as the church claimed they were.

Granted, the science-faith issue is a major instigator of doubt, but it's not the biggest. That distinction would have to go to the problem of suffering and evil. You come into work, check headlines on CNN online, and read about another schoolyard shooting, or see photos of the latest earthquake in Turkey or Taiwan, or replay the collapse of the Trade Towers, and you can't help but ask yourself how a good and all-powerful God could let these terrible things happen.

Another big doubt inspirer: bad behavior among Christians and churches. The shoddy behavior of the religious never fails to raise pointed doubts about the legitimacy of the Christian faith.

Another: what happens to people who don't believe? It feels so unjust and uncompassionate when some Christians glibly consign most of the human race to hell. Sensitive Christians feel there must be a better answer.

Short, easy answers are the last thing these doubts and questions need. If you brought such doubts to me, to do them justice would involve us forging an authentic relationship and engaging in real conversation—not merely a couple of hours over coffee. This is a lengthy process. I'd begin by affirming the good thing that you are after—truth, authenticity, honesty, compassion, justice. Then, instead of *answering* your doubts, I'd help you devise a number of possible answers and help you create options. Then together we'd evaluate the options in the light of Scripture, of experience, of what we've read or heard from wise people.

In short, instead of providing easy answers for your doubts and questions, I'd try to come alongside you as a companion in the search for those good things—truth, honesty, justice, and all the rest. And (this is perhaps the most important step) I'd try to help you keep praying through the process—because ultimately, faith isn't just about answers or concepts. Faith is about admitting that many of life's greatest truths are going to remain mysteries to us, due to the limitations of our tiny brains that weigh less than a cantaloupe. Faith is about reaching out to God to guide us, and asking for God's help so we can be honest, good-hearted seekers. That's what child-like faith is, in my opinion. It's not gullibility or intellectual laziness, but asking questions and having an insatiable curiosity for truth. It's reaching out to someone who knows more than we do.

This is why I am convinced that doubt can be a doorway to spiritual growth. Unfortunately, like most avenues of growth, it is often painful. Intellectual pain is an underrated cost of following Christ. If I didn't care about following Christ, I wouldn't care so much about being honest, seeking truth, or facing reality. I would be more tempted to simply go with the flow, take the easy way, maybe anesthetize my intellectual pain instead of persevering through it toward the truth.

If you're going through that kind of intellectual pain right now, lay it before God. The kind of dependence on God that you are exercising now, in the midst of intellectual uncertainty and confusion, may be the purest kind of faith found on planet earth. It involves an act of will and courage that I think must be far more valuable than we normally realize. It may even be heroic.

If you're in intellectual pain, find a circle of friends with whom you can be transparently honest. In a college dorm years ago I poured out my doubts to a good friend. I was doubting the Bible, Jesus, the value of the church, the possibility of miracles, the whole thing. He listened to everything, then said, "Brian, right now, none of this looks real to you. But sitting across the desk from you is a friend whose faith is strong right now, and I can see that God is bigger than your doubts. So if you need to, you can rely on my faith for a while, and I know we'll get through this together." His presence and friendship helped me outlast my low tide of faith.

Finally, if you are in intellectual pain or grave doubt or whatever kind of low tide of faith, try this: step up to a new level of Christian thinking by reading or listening to some new voices. The fact that your faith is struggling means you need some new teachers. When you're doubt, accept the challenge to think more, not less—to think deeper, not shallower. This might mean you're ready for C. S. Lewis and Peter Kreeft, Philip Yancey and Romano Guardini, Lesslie Newbigin and Nancey Murphy, St. Augustine and Blaise Pascal, Leo Tolstoy and Fyodor Dostoyevsky, Walker Percy and Thomas Merton, Stan Grenz, and Dallas Willard. A mind that stretches to embrace a new idea, it is said, never shrinks back to its previous dimensions. In times of doubt, there's no way around it: you're going to have to do some stretching.

But isn't this the way it ought to be? Shouldn't a growing Christian have a growing understanding? Isn't a vibrant, honest, tested faith worth some intellectual pain? Faith seems to grow in a kind of iterative, ascending spiral of four stages:

Simplicity. Everything is easy, black and white, known or knowable.

Complexity. The scenario has gotten more complex, so now you focus on techniques of finding the truth.

Perplexity. You become a disillusioned learner. You doubt all absolutes, all authority figures. Everything seems relative and hazy.

Maturity. A friend has pointed out that this stage would be better called *humility*, because in this stage you come to terms with your limitations and learn to live with mystery—not as a cop-out, but as an honest realization that only God understands everything. You carry out of stage four a shorter list of tested and cherished beliefs than you entered faith with back in *simplicity*. A lot of your previous dogmas that you grasped tightly, you now hold lightly and loosely.

In a sense a person keeps finding faith and then becoming frustrated with it and in a sense losing it, and then finding a better version of it, and so on—something like a software upgrade.

At least that's what has happened for me. At this stage in my life, I have sifted and re-sifted. Some beliefs I've released, others have proven themselves as keepers. This is where Jesus is so wonderful and helpful to a person whose faith is in low tide:

Jesus looked at the whole religious system of the Pharisees, which was enormously complex and full of inconsistencies, and he doubted the whole thing. He sifted out a lot of clutter and boiled all the rest down to elegant and livable essentials: love God with all your heart, mind, soul, and strength, and your neighbor as yourself. I would rather be sure of those few essentials and live by them, than be sure of a million fine points of systematic theology, and not live by Christ's call to love.

Sometimes I think our churches are like California, built on a San Andreas fault of suppressed doubt. Underneath the surface, the pressure of doubt that remains unexpressed and unresolved builds and builds, and sooner or later the landscape cracks and crumbles. Our current situation is only intensified by the precarious transition we find ourselves in now between a waning modern world and an emerging postmodern one. We have all been discipled in a thoroughly modern version of Christianity, yet here we are in the middle of a transition to a *postmodern* world. As a result, our modern apologetics and systematic theologies seem less relevant to those of us who are more postmodern people. That's why I believe we are approaching a time of real upheaval, with people raising new postmodern questions that modern Christians haven't answered yet—or even asked, for that matter.

But here's where faith comes in—a faith that leans on God, not on our theology. We have the challenge of believing that good answers are out there, if we only have the courage to press through the intellectual pain of questioning, seeking, learning, and stretching. I believe Jesus when he said he'll never leave us or forsake us—and that includes even when we question. Or as St. Paul said, even when we are faithless, God remains faithful. It's ironic: the more free I am to doubt a specific belief, the more free I become to hold on to that person-to-Person faith in God. At the point where the tide of faith seems the lowest, if we hang on and don't give up, we'll see the tide rise again.

After all, to trust our beliefs about God more than we trust God—wouldn't that be missing the point?

There seems to be a dialectic at work in what Brian writes—insightfully, I think—with the thesis being faith, the antithesis being doubt, and the synthesis being a faith that is tempered by doubt. Lord Tennyson once said, "There lies more faith in honest doubt than in half their creeds."

The operative phrase in Tennyson's statement is, of course, *honest doubt*. For much doubt is *dishonest* doubt. Philosopher and mathematician Blaise Pascal contended that most doubt comes from disobedience to God rather than through intellectual questioning. Pascal understood that if a person is raised in a religious tradition that forbids this or that behavior, and then enters into that behavior willfully and knowing that it is wrong, such a person will experience what psychologists now call *cognitive dissonance*. In other words, there will be tension in a person between what is believed and what is practiced.

Resolving that tension means repenting of the practice that contradicts the beliefs (the generally recommended course for Christians), or else changing one's beliefs to fit the behavior.

Which was poignantly illustrated when a student walked into my office one day to tell me he no longer believed in God. How long had he been shacking up with his girlfriend, I asked. Angry at first, he eventually admitted that, yes, he *was* sleeping with his girlfriend, although he said he couldn't see what *that* had to do with his intellectual doubts about the existence of God. I pointed out that the God he believes in doesn't allow him to exploit women sexually; and because he enjoys that behavior, he is attempting to jettison the God who would condemn his behavior. This student's doubt is not the result of intellectual reflection, but of disobeying the norms of his beliefs.

Those of us in pastoral ministry, leading youth groups, and teaching religion in academic settings can waste a lot of time trying to justify faith intellectually—when the fact is that those with whom we are arguing don't want to believe in God and the Scriptures because they would have to give up this or that pleasure or behavior.

Of course, there are certainly situations that do indeed make it nearly impossible to believe. Some of my Jewish friends contend that the Holocaust made it impossible for them to believe in a loving and powerful God who ruled the universe. Auschwitz made faith impossible for many Jews. What is amazing is that in the midst of such suffering, there are those whose faith somehow emerged triumphant— which only goes to show that faith is indeed a gift of God, as the Bible says.

Doubt can also be traced to biophysical factors. William James, one of the founders of psychology of religion, wrote in *The Varieties of Religious Experience* that there are some people who are "sick minded." He did not use that term in a derogatory sense, but was simply saying that there are some people, who because of biophysical factors, live in a state of depression and doubt. Who are genetically disposed to negativism. Who are skeptical and even cynical by nature. Who are "down" all the time because of biophysical reasons. Sometimes this condition becomes so severe that medication becomes necessary, and perhaps even institutionalization. (It is at this point that I really get into the charismatic movement and believe that sometimes a strong outpouring of the Holy Spirit into the life of a "sick-minded" person is what is needed to deliver them into a joyful faith.)

Brian is absolutely right when he contends that a faith that is not tested by doubt is a faith that leaves the individual vulnerable. We

229

have seen young men and women go off to universities with a naïve version of Christianity that has never been questioned. They are so vulnerable to the confrontations in the classroom and the dorm that their survival as Christians is in jeopardy.

If we can go through periods of doubt without being destroyed by it, we will be made stronger. Doubt is the fire that purifies our faith. Doubt burns up the hay, wood, and stubble, leaving behind pure gold.

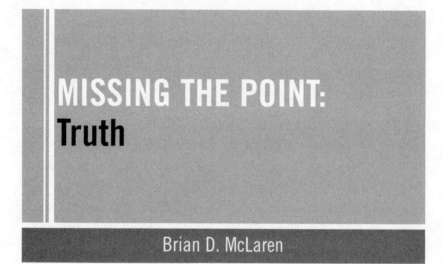

MISSING THE POINT:
Truth

Brian D. McLaren

If I could go back and live another life or two, I would spend one of them as a scientist in the mold of Dian Fossey, Jane Goodall, or Birute Galdikas—familiar names to readers of *National Geographic*. Trained by the renowned Dr. Louis Leakey, these three scientists left his tutelage to study gorillas, chimpanzees, and orangutans (respectively). You may recall the *National Geographic* photos of Goodall, for example, leaning against the trunk of a tree, the chimpanzees, having grown accustomed to her presence, gamboling about—chewing on twigs, romping and screaming, nursing, mating, and otherwise hanging out chimp style. There sits Goodall, ponytailed, trim in her khaki shirt and shorts, notebook in hand, motionless as a stump, observing the chimps of Gombe as if she were in a lab staring down through a microscope at paramecia.

This is the classic pose of the scientist in the modern world: the objective observer, taking notes, detached, cool, transcendent, like *Star Trek* scientists following the Prime Directive: observation only, no participation, no interference. What she sees, whether through the eyepiece of a microscope or with her naked eyes, is utterly objective—that is, it is an *object* to be observed by a *subject*.

But the story of Goodall (or of Fossey or Galdikas) doesn't stop there. You have to imagine a moment one day when a young chimp ambles over to Goodall and looks deep into her eyes and holds out her hand and Goodall, abandoning her own Prime Directive, reaches out her hand and—in a moment reminiscent of Michelangelo's Sistine Chapel ceiling fresco—the two primates touch, fingertip to fingertip. The touch is not the handling of a specimen by a scientist, not the touch of a subject and an object. It is the touch of two knowing creatures—two subjects—who have entered into a relationship. Like a puppy being wagged by its enthusiastic tail, bounding breathless, loping to a boy with a stick in its mouth (*Let's play!*

233

Okay? Okay?), the young chimp seems to say to the scientist, "Let's be friends! I am inviting you out of your objective invisibility to become a visible part of my world, where you as a subject and I as a subject may interact in a relationship of mutuality." And Goodall extends her hand, and by her gesture says, *Yes. I accept your invitation. Let's be friends.*

Of course the chimp didn't say this—but Goodall's description of the moment makes it clear that something very much like this did happen:

As David [Greybeard, the chimp] and I sat there, I noticed a ripe red fruit from an oil nut palm lying on the ground. I held it toward him on the palm of my hand. David glanced at me and reached to take the nut. He dropped it, but gently held my hand. I needed no words to understand his message of reassurance: he didn't want the nut, but he understood my motivation, he knew I meant well. To this day I remember the soft pressure of his fingers. We had communicated in a language far more ancient than words, a language that we shared with our prehistoric ancestor, a language bridging our two worlds. And I was deeply moved. When David got up and walked away I let him go and stayed there quietly by the murmuring stream, holding on to the experience so that I could know it in my heart forever. (Jane Goodall, *Reason for Hope*)

It's an amazing moment, really. Members of two species of higher primates entered a new kind of relationship: not hunter-prey, farmer-farmed, circus trainer-trainee, owner-pet, or even scientist-object of study. Rather than subject-object, they become subject-subject. Friend-friend. American author Walker Percy and others have called this move from an I-it relationship to an I-thou relationship *intersubjectivity*, a useful term that distinguishes itself both from objectivity (where I am a detached, disinterested, transcendent, abstracted knower) and from subjectivity (where I am self-engrossed, caught up in my own biases, desires, and perspectives).

And along the intersubjective way, Goodall does something horribly unscientific. She doesn't describe this chimp as *Pan troglodytes* or Female-7 or #3C1f. To this researcher the chimp becomes David Greybeard—and the others Ferdinand, Fifi, Flo, Freud, Frodo, Goblin, Mike, Goliath, Flint, Passion, and Pam. A name. What one subject typically gives to another subject. The relationship between two named beings is seldom utilitarian, objective, detached, or scientific—but rather personal, friendly, mutual, exploratory.

And the relationship between Goodall and her named subjects grew deeper. Here the scientist described her decision to violate normal scientific protocol:

AT THAT TIME I WAS LEARNING MORE AND MORE ABOUT THE CHIMPANZEES. AS I GOT TO KNOW THEM AS INDIVIDUALS, I NAMED THEM. I HAD NO IDEA THAT THIS, ACCORDING TO THE ETHOLOGICAL DISCIPLINE OF THE EARLY 1960S, WAS INAPPROPRIATE—I SHOULD HAVE GIVEN THEM MORE OBJECTIVE NUMBERS. I ALSO DESCRIBED THEIR VIVID PERSONALITIES—ANOTHER SIN: ONLY HUMANS HAD PERSONALITIES. IT WAS AN EVEN WORSE CRIME TO ATTRIBUTE HUMANLIKE EMOTIONS TO THE CHIMPANZEES.... FORTUNATELY, I HAD NOT BEEN TO UNIVERSITY, AND I DID NOT KNOW THESE THINGS. AND WHEN I DID FIND OUT, I JUST THOUGHT IT WAS

Horrifically, some years later poachers killed David
Greybeard and others of his clan. And true to a subject-subject
relationship, Goodall doesn't merely record in her diary: "4
Pan troglodytes found deceased and decapitated in jungle approx.
2.4 km NNE of base camp. Hands cut off, apparently by
machete." No, she weeps—and not because her research project
is set back and polluted by human interference. She weeps as a
woman, as a subjective human being, because her inter*subjective*
friends have been *objectively* killed, and she feels a moral
outrage, a betrayal by her own species, a blatant injustice.

So she moves one step further beyond objectivity. Now she
is nowhere near a detached scientist, a cool observer, an
objective subject observing objective objects. Now Goodall gets
on a plane for Washington and London and wherever she can
raise consciousness and money for a cause: to save and protect
her friends, and the friends of her friends, the chimpanzees.
This is no longer "pure" science: it becomes a story, a journey,
an adventure, a crusade, a passion. This is something
postscientific, postobjective. This is love.

Objectivity has great value. But like analysis, in the modern
world it became a kind of narcotic to us. We seemed to believe
that, ultimately, objectivity was the only way to be (perhaps
because as a culture we were edging God out, instead
envisioning a mechanical, impersonal, purposeless universe).
Like *Star Trek's* Spock, we believed that cool, emotion-free,
objective logic would be our salvation.

But it didn't turn out that way for most of us on this side of modernity. We feel more like Data of *Star Trek: The Next Generation*: we want to be more human, more emotional, more involved, less detached and mechanistic. Sure, scientific objectivity was a good step for us, necessary to our growth and development. But objectivity wasn't the final step.

For Christians in particular, our faith must always draw us beyond objectivity, because there is no sphere of life where we live as pure, abstracted, uninvolved subjects who objectify the world. To the contrary: whether voting, raising children, cooking goose stew, cutting the lawn, rolling on deodorant, sitting in traffic, counting tomatoes in our garden, making love, studying chimpanzees or paramecia—in every sphere of our humanity we find ourselves as beings-in-relationship with that which we interact. We live, move, and have our being in relationships, because God the ultimate reality is at heart a triune relational being. What's more, God the ultimate subject has created us for an intersubjective relationship with himself, with one another, and with creation.

The ramifications of this post-objective shift are staggering. The universe changes from a collection of objects to be observed, used, exploited, and studied to an environment full of creations that actually demand something of me as a fellow creature: the beauty of a wildflower demands that I appreciate it...the fragility of a wolf or warbler population, or of an endangered insect species demands that I conserve it...the potential of an aquifer or of a vein of ore demands that I use it wisely...the vastness of wilderness demands that I explore it.

This shift from object to subject also demands a change in my role in the universe. I as a human am no longer the sovereign top of the food chain, using an objectified world however I want to. No, I and all creation are loved by and accountable to the watchful eye of God, who, as Supreme

Subject does not objectify reality (that is, does not render reality as objects to be used and discarded), but rather forms creations of dignity—who are themselves not mere objects, but real, bona fide, dignified subjects. I see that I am created for intersubjective relationships—that is, for love—with other creations and with the Creator as well. And suddenly love moves from being a sentimental illusion (as it was in the naturalistic view of modernity) to the main point of everything.

What could any of this possibly have to do with being people who orient their lives around faith, God, and mission? A lot. Consider these specifics:

The Goal of Theology

What was the goal of theology in the modern era, other than this: to describe God as a scientist describes an object—objective, detached, sanitized of subjectivity, removed from the variable of personal relationship? Do you see how fundamentally absurd this seems in a post-modern world, where the most obvious fact about a creature is that he always, at every minute, exists as a subject in intersubjective relation to God the ultimate Subject, and therefore can never be objective in dealing with God? For a new kind of Christian, there is no objective laboratory (seminary, study, pulpit) where we can remove the subjective "variables" of who we are, and where we are; rather, those very variables are essential factors in how we see God, life, ourselves, everything. The form of the Bible suddenly makes more sense, being comprised, as it is, of 100 percent stories, poetry, personal letters, et cetera, all linked to concrete environments and very human authors with all their messy variables ... not even .01 percent of the Bible presenting itself as situation-sanitized, abstracted, objective information about God.

This "messy" form of the Bible was an embarrassment to us in the modern era; we would have much preferred a Bible more akin to a scientific textbook, legal code, or encyclopedia. But in the emerging culture, we see the motley patchwork form of the Bible itself as one of its most important messages: that God comes to us not as a subject to objects, nor yet as an object under study yielding to us as studying subjects, but rather that God comes to us in inter-subjectivity, in relationship, in history, in an environment, in the stuff of our day to day lives.

Christianity's Claims to Truth

How were the truth-claims of Christianity presented in the modern era, other than as objective facts, historically or scientifically verifiable (we hoped), as abstract absolutes, as a kind of impersonal third party intruding upon our subjective experience with objective information? For a new kind of Christian, these kinds of objective truth-claims still must have great value, but we acknowledge the additional value of other kinds of truth-claims...those that modern folk may have dismissed as being subjective, but which we will assert are in fact inter-subjective...meaning that they manifest themselves to us a real experiences with God. For example, instead of offering a list of objective evidences and then demanding a verdict, we go on to offer a story that can't be objectively proven, but which can subjectively ring true and make sense of our lives.

The Propagation of the Gospel

How was the gospel preached in the modern era, if not as "Four Spiritual Laws" (like the objective laws of science—the highest reality we could imagine!) or "Steps to Peace with God" (like technical directions containing information needed to perform a repeatable experiment, steps which, when followed, will yield the expected result with scientific precision)? For a new kind of Christian, while these formulae may still have some usefulness, we are always suspicious of them, because whether they are presented as laws of physics or technical directions ... they may reduce and truncate the very gospel they are trying to contain and transmit, like a cheap radio trying to broadcast a live symphonic performance, or a sound bite trying to report a full, many-faceted news event.

Detached Analysis

How was the Bible generally studied in the modern era, if not as a dissected rat or frog (that is, an object) in a laboratory (or classroom), by people who denied their subjectivity (scholars), in an attempt to salvage the abstract principles from any context (like an objective scientific principle) so they could be applied (that is, used, as a technique or scientific formula) to any situation (regardless of its subjective, personal, relational context)?

In spite of all the ways in which liberals and conservatives disagreed about biblical interpretation in the modern era, do you begin to see how they were modern brothers in this way ... that when they were acting as scholars (objective investigators), they were aspiring to an abstracted posture of objectivity, as subjects (denying their subjectivity) who stood detached, outside and above the text—not as people in an environment, a predicament, people who are at every moment in relation to the God whose name salts the pages of the Bible?

Novelist Walker Percy has explored this theme in many of his essays, including "The Man on the Train," "The Loss of the Creature," and "The Message in the Bottle." In these essays a man on a train looks at his hand...a high school student studies a dogfish...a castaway reads bottle-encapsulated messages. Each of them realizes in his or her own way exactly what we're exploring here: that I exist in relation to everything else—that I am not just an impersonal, objective abstraction, nor a mere organism in an environment. I am a person in a predicament, a mess, a situation where I need to make choices without all the data I might wish for—like Dorothy in *The Wizard of Oz*, realizing that she's not in Kansas any more. As a person in a predicament, I cannot fade "into the furniture of the It," as Percy puts it. I cannot be the abstracted observer, still as a stump, taking notes.

This realization changes everything. Listen to Percy imagine a classroom where fish, trees, shells, people, or dreams are studied in an objective, modern way from his book, *The Message in the Bottle*:

THE DOGFISH, THE TREE, THE SEASHELL, THE AMERICAN NEGRO, THE DREAM, ARE RENDERED INVISIBLE BY A SHIFT OF REALITY FROM CONCRETE THING TO THEORY WHICH WHITEHEAD HAS CALLED THE FALLACY OF MISPLACED CONCRETENESS. IT IS THE MISTAKING OF AN IDEA, A PRINCIPLE, AN ABSTRACTION, FOR THE REAL. AS A CONSEQUENCE OF THE SHIFT, THE "SPECIMEN" IS SEEN AS LESS REAL THAN THE THEORY OF THE SPECIMEN. AS KIERKEGAARD SAID, ONCE A PERSON IS SEEN AS A SPECIMEN OF A RACE OR A SPECIES, AT THAT VERY MOMENT HE CEASES TO BE AN INDIVIDUAL. THEN THERE ARE NO MORE INDIVIDUALS BUT ONLY SPECIMENS.... (P. 58)

[THE LAYMAN] BELIEVES THAT THE THING [A DOGFISH, SEASHELL, AN ARCHEOLOGICAL ARTIFACT, AMERICAN NEGRO, AN OAK TREE] IS DISPOSED OF BY THEORY, THAT IT STANDS IN THE PLATONIC RELATION OF BEING A SPECIMEN OF SUCH AND SUCH AN UNDERLYING

PRINCIPLE. IN THE TRANSMISSION OF SCIENTIFIC THEO-
RY FROM THEORIST TO LAYMAN, THE EXPECTATION OF
THE THEORIST IS REVERSED. INSTEAD OF THE MARVELS
OF THE UNIVERSE BEING MADE AVAILABLE TO THE PUB-
LIC, THE UNIVERSE IS DISPOSED OF BY THEORY. THE
LOSS OF SOVEREIGNTY TAKES THIS FORM: AS A RESULT
OF THE SCIENCE OF BOTANY, TREES ARE NOT MADE
AVAILABLE TO EVERY MAN. ON THE CONTRARY. THE
TREE LOSES ITS PROPER DENSITY AND MYSTERY AS A
CONCRETE EXISTENT AND, AS MERELY ANOTHER SPECI-
MEN OF A SPECIES, BECOMES ITSELF NUGATORY. (P. 63)

When trees, artifacts, dogfish, or even my own hand become merely another specimen, this is a shame. But when the entire universe loses its density, as Percy puts it—and when God himself becomes "nugatory" by objectification—and when one loses even the sense of his own, actual, predicamental existence and fades into the furniture of the It—then one begins yearning for modernity to give way to something better. Then one begins yearning for a new kind of world, a new kind of Christian.

One of my maxims is this: In the process of being against something worth being against, one often becomes for something not worth being for. Case in point: whenever I turn on a Christian radio broadcast or visit a Christian bookstore these days, I hear or read preacher after preacher beating the drum of Absolute Truth, as if the term was on the same level as repentance, salvation, prayer, God, love—as if it were part of the vocabulary of the Bible. I appreciate that these Christian brothers and sisters of mine are against something worth being against—the loss of moral passion and virtue, the loss of vibrant faith, the eclipse of spiritual conviction in a kind of thin relativistic fog.

But what are they *for*? Is it possible that the Absolute Truth they defend is not in the end worth being for? Or at least not worth nearly as much as our own biblical story?

What if our love affair with the idea of absolute or objective truth reflects not a presumed biblical orthodoxy as much as it does our modern Western mindset? Is it possible that even our idea of absolute truth is simply another objectification, another "loss of the creature," another rendering of reality (warm and quivering and pulsing with life and meaning and specificity) into a "nugatory"?

And maybe in defending our modern idea of absolute truth, we not only align ourselves against something worth being against, but in the bargain find ourselves arguing for things *not* worth arguing for.

It's not that I am recommending something less than objectivity—to the contrary, I'm recommending something *more*. I am all for objectivity, absolute truth, and propositions. I'm simply pointing out that—after 500 years of objectifying everything, and de-subjectifying ourselves, and pursuing absolute truth whether scientific or religious—we now see modernity for what it is: simultaneously a blessing (have you taken an antibiotic or boarded an airplane lately?) and a curse.

All of which means this: that we as Christians can no longer approach the Bible as if we were in a laboratory, seeking for abstract, universal principles devoid of contexts and environments, believing we can approach the text objectively, as if we were stumps or furniture or zeroes. Impossible. We cannot help but approach the Bible as subjects encountering a subject, with our background, prejudices, assumptions, biases, needs, misunderstandings, experiences—in a word, our subjectivities—intact. And with our respect for the subjectivities of the writers intact, too.

And more: we Christians can acknowledge that our subjectivity in approaching the Bible is in fact not a bad thing, it does not compromise our spirituality or our understanding of the Bible or our orthodoxy. Such subjectivity is actually necessary—it is a reality that even the Bible itself assumes, for it is a premodern text and therefore less addicted to objectivity. Any attempts of ours to read the Bible objectively are actually modern invasions into our reading.

So we need to become a new kind of post-objective, intersubjective Christian in several ways.

- We must complement the value of a cool head with a warm heart.

- We must see that analytical thinking without appropriate passion is as unbalanced as passion without consideration.

- We must realize that the chimps and gorillas and orangutans of this world must not only be studied, but also loved; and when threatened, saved—and not just primates, but everything that God has created.

- We must walk into church as subjects in a predicament—not as an abstracted physicist listening to a lecture, but as a castaway on a desert island finding bottles on the beach with notes inside about how to survive, how to find rescue.

- We must open the Bible as persons in need of God, reading a book that has helped other people in their predicaments.

- We must perceive ourselves as part of the story that the Bible celebrates—and celebrates in all of its varied and specific contexts, eras, situations, and milieus.

- We must never let ourselves believe the fantasy that we can crawl out of our skin and speak of either the Creator or any creature from a posture of anything other than what we are: ourselves creatures, part of creation, related to every other creature, and standing in intersubjective relation to the Creator, be the relation friendly or hostile, submissive or rebellious, loving or indifferent.

- We must admit that our quest for ultimate and absolute truth is impossible, if not for the reasons postmodern philosophers raise, then for this reason: the ultimate truth is not an objective concept, not an objective principle, but rather a Person, the Subject of such splendor, dignity, wonder, winsomeness, and glory that to know him is to love him, worship him, enjoy him, and seek to please him with one's very existence. When God comes to us, God doesn't say, "Seek for absolute, objective, propositional truth," but rather, "I am the way, the truth, the life."

How different would our preaching, theologizing, worshipping, studying, evangelizing, debating, dividing, polemicizing, neighboring, and pontificating be if we stopped missing the point about reality—if we moved beyond objectivity instead of stopping there—if we became more mindful of our intersubjective situation as participants in God's amazing story of relationships made, broken, and reconciled?

Brian makes such a good point about the importance of the subjective encounter with God that he tends, I think, to minimize the importance of the objective truths of the Scriptures.

Unlike Brian, I believe that objective, propositional, ultimate truth is of absolute importance. If, for example, an archaeologist were to discover the remains of Jesus, I am convinced that Christianity would fade away and the church would collapse. The whole salvation story evaporates unless there was an actual Jesus who actually died on the cross for our sins and who actually came back from the grave. The Scriptures themselves make a point in establishing the objective validity of such claims by telling us, among other things, exactly who witnessed the resurrection and how many people could testify to the resurrection.

We ought not to follow those "modern scholars," Brian writes, who abstract principles from the stories and various declarations of the Bible and then apply those principles in contemporary settings to inform us how to believe and act. But that's *exactly* what I think we should be doing.

For me, the tension between objective and subjective truth was set in motion by the people at the good old fundamentalist church where I grew up. They hammered away at the propositional aspect of the gospel and ferociously defended the objective validity of the Bible— yet they knew that believing these tenets was no substitute for having a personal, subjective relationship with Christ. I remember my simple,

Bible-preaching pastor declaring. "You can hold the right theology, but unless you know Jesus personally, you're lost!"

MISSING THE POINT:
Being Postmodern

Brian D. McLaren

Let's talk about the term *postmodern.*

Nearly everybody is sick of it. And no wonder, since it is used in a jillion different ways. In many Christian circles both conservative and liberal, *postmodern* means nihilistic, relativistic, anti-Christian, and otherwise slimy and bad. (As if the term *modern* were so much more hospitable to Christian faith!) Even among those who are more sophisticated in their understanding of the term, there is still a suspicion that if we aren't careful, we'll sell out and conform to whatever *postmodern* is, and thus prove unfaithful to the gospel. (As if we had the alternative of a culture-free version of the gospel, or as if we weren't already conformed in many ways to modernity.)

After 9/11 it was fashionable to say, "See? People are waving flags again. Ha! Postmodernism is dead!" This was probably wishful thinking by those who hoped that postmodernism would be a phase, and we'd get back to good old sensible modernity soon enough.

Some folks point out things that don't appear to be changing, like the power of consumerism, and conclude that what we now have is not postmodernity, but rather hypermodernity.

Some folks have started multiplying the *post's*, so we have post-postmodernism and post-post-postmodernism.

For others, the term postmodern became a banner, label, or slogan—sometimes divisively. Mistaking a profound cultural and philosophical shift for a shallow stylistic fad, people talk about starting "postmodern church services" and having "postmodern churches." What do they mean? Same old concepts, same old attitudes, but now with candles (wow!) and edgier music (cool!) and flannel shirts (yeah!) with some goatees and art thrown in. In this context, *traditional worship* means *uncool* (i.e., suitable for the over-50 crowd), *contemporary worship* means used to be cool (suitable for the over-35 crowd), and *postmodern* means *really cool* (suitable for the under-35 crowd).

For all these reasons and more, I'm sick of the term too—and I'm even more sick of all the stupid arguments about it, and I'm sicker still of post-post-posties. It's enough to make a person go postal.

But I will still use the term—not because of stubbornness, but because I think it's the best term we have so far. And actually, I think the term is still as helpful as it is annoying.

Consider the Middle Ages of Europe, the historical period stretching from about the fall of Rome to the Protestant Reformation—from A.D. 500 to 1500 or so. This era wasn't born in a day, but rather emerged over centuries. Medieval themes developed over a long period of time—and so did counter-themes. No one single event—not even the fall of Rome—launched the medieval era. No one could say, "Today begins the Middle Ages." Nevertheless, when a number of themes seemed to come together in the Mediterranean world, as they began to synergize and cohere, so that the era seemed to take on a certain ethos and trajectory and shape and life of its own—then the medieval world gradually emerged: a culture dominated by the church, organized around a developing feudal economy, self-perceived within a Ptolemaic cosmology, picking up the pieces after the fall of the old Roman Empire, coping with invading tribes from nearly every direction, and surviving wave after wave of plagues.

Similarly, the modern world wasn't born in a day. But there was another convergence of themes and technologies and beginnings—the printing press, the caravel, the rifle, the Copernican model of the universe, the challenge to the church's authority by German political leaders and insolent priests. Interestingly, the term *modern* was first used in the 1490s, when scholars began calling the previous era *middle*.

People seemed to feel that something was different, even though they couldn't have predicted exactly what shape the emerging modern era would take.

In many ways, the modern era didn't fully arrive until the Enlightenment in the mid-1600s. It developed gradually but surely over time, and continued growing and developing until today.

In some ways, in fact, we have four worlds coexisting on our planet today:

- There are still *prehistoric* pockets in a few rainforests.

- There are (or have been until very recently) *medieval* warlords and feudal economies in places like Afghanistan.

- There are, of course, huge *modern* economies and institutions and governments, and millions who feel at home in them.

- And, as I maintain in this chapter, there are signs of something *beyond modernity* too.

As I see it, emerging paradigms typically begin with a negative tone. At first just a few people become angry with the status quo. They protest, critique, and complain about the current paradigm. Some of them eventually start trying to articulate something better even as the stage they're protesting continues—because it takes time to distance oneself enough from the dominant culture so that one can begin to see any creative alternatives.

Those who speak of *post-postmodernism* are, I think, assuming that postmodern means only this early negative phase. I'd rather refer to this early negative phase of postmodern culture as "the early negative phase of postmodern culture." That will save having to add a lot of *posts* as new phases come along.

251

(By the way, I expect that some people in the early negative phase will paint themselves into a corner and become not postmodern, but antimodern. First, they may advocate a return to some idyllic, premodern past that, of course, never existed and to which, therefore, no one can ever return. Second, they may become so fiercely opposed to modernity that they refuse to use the accumulated and valuable capital of modernity. They'll throw out the baby with the bath water, the worthwhile lessons and benefits of modernity with its shortcomings and disadvantages. And deprived of the baby modernity, antimodern movements won't get very far.)

A lot of people seem to think that since modernity was rationalistic, postmodernity must be either antirational or irrational. No, that's antimodernity, not postmodernity. Postmodernity more likely seeks to integrate rationality with things *beyond* rationality—things like imagination, intuition, and faith. In fact, if the medieval era is seen as an era of faith (in a Hegelian progression, the thesis), and the modern era as an era of reason (the antithesis), we could expect the postmodern era to be a synthesis of faith *and* reason. (Primatologist Jane Goodall hinted hopefully at this synthesis when she said, "If you think the Age of Reason was good, just wait until you see the Age of Love.")

Furthermore, since modernity was all about progress and optimism, then (some conclude) postmodernity will be about despair and pessimism. Not quite. Early modernity was perhaps more generally optimistic about human progress. But late modernity (after World War II) became cynical, jaded, disillusioned about progress—at least among most intellectuals. Postmodernity, I expect, will emerge as something both optimistic and pessimistic about progress—a synthesis, not a rejection.

252

Synthesis describes most cultures. Few cultures have been monolithic or homogenous. A culture, someone said, is a group of people who argue about the same things over generations. Say a culture believes that the tension between the rights of the individual and the good of the collective is an important issue: then that culture will be characterized by heterogeneity—that is, by argument. The fact that the individual-collective argument is an unresolved issue (as it is in our current culture) helps define that culture. It's the argument, the conversation, the not-reaching-agreement-about-the-issue that creates the culture.

Here's another tension: the modern era was largely rationalistic, but not without a strong romantic strain that *protested* rationalism. Thus modernity is best defined not by a monolithic opinion about reason, but rather by an ongoing argument about reason and its relationship to feeling, faith, et cetera.

Now here is where a culture takes on a postmodern cast: when we begin assuming that there is some sort of dynamic tension between reason and feeling, faith, et cetera, and stop expecting one side to ever win over the other. The old (modern) reason-feeling argument doesn't disappear, but it now becomes an *accepted* dynamic tension.

In other words, nobody wins the argument; we just get tired of it and have already said all that we can think of to say about it, so we more or less accept it as an unresolved issue that we can live with, and our attention moves on to some new questions or problems—perhaps, as Goodall suggested, in the direction of love: how do people of vastly differing belief systems get along on a small and increasingly interconnected planet?

Another reason for widespread fatigue with the term *postmodern*: people like me who talk about the subject too often

253

indulge in facile dualisms. This is so *modern*, we say with self-impressed arrogance, and that is so *postmodern*. Such facile contrast is not only annoying, it's stupid. I've heard people imply, for example, that planning is so distressingly modern, and spontaneity is so liberatingly postmodern.

Wrong. Planning and spontaneity are both human. They always exist where humans exist. True, there is a kind of modern fascination with mechanistic control and technique that leads to a kind of favored modern planning. But postmodern people who tire of the mechanistic control and technique cannot and should not abandon all planning; otherwise they will live like amnesiacs, with no memory of past lessons learned the hard way—and therefore no ideas for better future attempts (which require *plans*).

Postmodern people will simply develop *new* kinds of planning that are less about mechanistic control and technique—perhaps that preserve a planned-for margin to allow for spontaneity! In any case, *modern* planning may be modern, but there's nothing merely modern with planning itself.

By the way, as soon as someone comes up with a better term than *postmodern*, or even a mildly promising candidate for a better term, let me know. What we call the automobile or car was known as a horseless carriage for a while, but not forever; I fully expect *postmodern* to be replaced someday, just as *horseless carriage* was.

In the meantime, one of the reasons I haven't abandoned the term is this: the older I get, the more I think in longer time frames and the more I learn. So I see the postmodern transition as a 75- or 150-year process. I don't expect postmodernity to mature in my lifetime, so we might not figure out a more positive name for at least that long. I expect it will still be a fledgling, anonymous phenomenon when my kids retire. A time frame of several generations used to bother me, but now I realize that each of us, like David, must simply serve God in our generation, and then die (Acts 13:36). And then others will take up the baton (if we have passed the baton reasonably well), and on through successive generations. We don't need to name our times in order to use them in faithful service to God—although understanding them as well as we can makes sense to me.

One other reason I haven't given up on the term *postmodern*: I actually believe that common people of faith like you and me play a role in defining not just the term, but the era itself. I sense in this transition a desperate need for people of faith to enter the fray and help create a new postmodern synthesis. Just as medieval faith without modern reason didn't work, so modern reason without faith doesn't work, either. Maybe there's an untried alternative that we can help to pioneer...maybe we have come to the kingdom for such a time as this...maybe this opportunity is part of what keeps me hopeful about the times we are in, and that hopefulness keeps me using the term.

At any rate, postmodernity isn't going to be forced on anyone, at least not for a long time. I fully expect that, especially in the world of religion, modernity will stay strong for a few more centuries. Let's face it: there are still quite a few more or less medieval Roman Catholics out there, and quite a few more medieval Moslems. The world of religion has a way of sanctifying the last era and riding it until the next era is nearly over—a conservatism gives religion a bad name, as if God isn't quite strong or wise enough to deal with today.

Not that such theological conservatism is an entirely bad thing. After all, many of us postmoderns are rediscovering good things from our medieval heritage, things that modernity forgot, and we are learning to appreciate those who have maintained medieval values or practices through harsh modern climates. Similarly, I wouldn't put it past God to keep alive some modern treasures of faith for the benefit of future generations.

Remembering this just may save us from postmodern snobbery. I'd rather be a humble modern than a snobbish postmodern any day. Better yet, I'd rather be a humble Christian seeking to do God's will in our fast-changing world in harmony and collaboration with all God's people (whatever their taste in eras).

So if you just want to be postmodern, you're missing the point. That's just too easy of an aspiration: all you have to do is go with the flow of culture, and you'll probably get there. If you want a challenge, though, aim to follow Jesus in the world—really in it—but not of it, whether in its modern or postmodern forms. *That* uncharted adventure will take you a lot closer to the point.

Campolo Responds

As Brian suggests, postmodernism is impossible to define at this particular stage of its historical development (although plenty of sermons have been preached that define postmodernism only to condemn it). What's more, he makes the case that a postmodern mindset may not be antithetical to Christianity, but rather receptive to the gospel.

There is little doubt, for instance, that the rise of the charismatic movement in recent decades is due to the fact that it is a functional fit for a postmodern society. Charismatic Christianity offers dimensions to the Christian faith that transcend the cold and rigid parameters of rational, scientific, modern ways of thinking. The charismatic movement recognizes miracles and spiritual forces at work in the world—ideas that fall beyond the limits of modernistic thinking.

This represents a fundamental shift within evangelical Christianity over the last half century. When I was growing up, there was a strong emphasis on apologetics; it was thought that Christianity had to be integrated with rationalistic and scientific thinking, or else it would not be acceptable. It was feared that, torn between science and Christianity, students would give up Christianity. It never occurred to anyone that they just might give up on science—probably because modernism enthroned science. We had absolute confidence in what it claimed, and we believed that it would lead us into all truth.

Instead of being the great savior, however, science is increasingly perceived now as a kind of Frankenstein monster. Science-based technology has polluted the environment and created weapons of mass destruction, both of which threaten our very existence. Instead of science saving us, we are now looking to be saved from science.

And therein is an opportunity for those of us who preach the gospel to offer Christ as a countervailing hope for the threats of our technological positivistic world.

I also appreciated how Brian reminded us that even in the modern era, artists—poets, painters, sculptors, architects—portrayed a transmodern reality, a reality that was beyond the merely mathematical and empirical dimensions. Even in the middle of modernism—in the early part of the 20th century—it was artists who let us know that a postmodern era was on its way. And now it remains for us Christians to pay attention to the arts so we can know what's coming, and so we can prepare ourselves to address the mindset that is emerging even now, and will come to dominate our thinking for several generations to come.

Concerning what Brian writes about progress: it should be noted that Christianity has its own very specific belief in progress. Bible-believing Christians know that history is going somewhere. It started in a garden, and it will end in the City of God. No reading of the Bible can leave any doubt that there is a progressive quality to the historic process. But unlike the liberalism of the early part of the 20th century, most evangelicals know that the kingdom of God will not be realized through human efforts alone. With theologians of hope like Jürgen Moltmann, we believe in Christ joining the church at the Second Coming, so that the good work that is being initiated in us will be completed on that great day (Philippians 1:6). History will not end with a bang or a whimper. We know that the kingdoms of this world will become the kingdom of our God, and that God shall reign forever and ever.

In short, belief in progress—to believe that there is a *telos* to history—is not necessarily a modernistic trait. Postmodernism isn't sure about the future. Christianity is! As my dear mother used to tell me, we do not know what the future holds, but we know who holds the future. We know that God can be trusted to bring all things to a glorious fruition.